Mockingbird's Song

Arnold Heflin

Mockingbird's Song

Hettie Keller's 10 Maxims for Peace and Happiness

Arnold Heflin

Arnold Heflin

This book is dedicated to my children,

Dianne and Craig,

who have taught me about love and courage.

Arnold Heflin

CONTENTS

Chapter One	1
Chapter Two	16
Chapter Three	28
Chapter Four	37
Chapter Five	50
Chapter Six	62
Chapter Seven	73
Chapter Eight	86
Chapter Nine	97
Chapter Ten	109
Chapter Eleven	122
Chapter Twelve	131
Hettie Keller's 10 Maxims	143
Afterward	145
Acknowledgements	147
Pictures of Hettie Keller	149

Arnold Heflin

CHAPTER ONE

I saw my friend Hettie Keller every Saturday for four years, but she never saw me. Now I stood in a remote Georgia cemetery where five people had come to lay her to rest. The grass slumped toward the earth, parched by the July heat. A lone sound came from a mockingbird perched high above the funeral tent in the still branches of a loblolly pine. The modest gray casket lay ominous and final as the smell of damp red clay filled the air.

The preacher asked an elderly woman sitting in a folding chair next to me to sing Hettie's favorite song. She stood and turned toward me. I noticed she was blind like my friend. She began to sing, "Amazing grace how sweet the sound." Her clear notes surprised me for she was well into her eighties. She continued, "I once was blind, but now I see." I remember thinking, "Hettie can see me now," and my thoughts drifted back to the day we met.

In January of 1993 I drove sixty miles through an Atlanta winter downpour to meet her at a nursing home in an older section of the city. We had talked on the telephone earlier in the week, and she expected me to arrive at 11:30 with lunch for both of us. The weather delayed me, and I entered the front door to be greeted by a woman in her thirties wearing a white nurse's uniform. She was about six feet, somewhat heavy, and voluptuous. She had more curves than the back road to

1

Cartersville. She smiled as her brown hand engulfed mine in welcome. "My name is Caroline, but everyone calls me Carol," she said. "You must be Mr. Heflin. Mrs. Keller is waiting for you. The candy you sent made an impression because I have never seen her this excited. Let's hurry along and we'll get acquainted later." I followed her from the kitchen through the dining room where the scent of bacon lingered. Carol stopped and pointed toward the den.

I entered the room and saw a woman in a loose-fitting green dress sitting alone, barely visible inside a brown overstuffed chair. Her child-size feet dangled several inches above the floor. A white cane with a red tip leaned against the chair, and a black book in her lap covered her body from her waist to her knees. She held both index fingers together and skimmed them across the pages, but her face was not lowered toward the book. She appeared to be staring straight ahead.

I paused to observe her, and I could not believe she was ninety-three-years old. She had high cheekbones and few wrinkles. Her skin was healthy and clear, and her lips full and pink under a prominent nose. Her eyebrows were bushy and dark, a sharp contrast to the silver hair cut short above her large ears. She looked as hardy as a juniper.

I walked over, leaned down and in my deepest Southern accent said, "Hello darling."

She raised her head toward the sound of my voice. "Is that you Rhett?" She giggled. "Have you come to take me to Charleston?" Our relationship began in laughter, and I reached down and shook her hand. "It's a pleasure to meet you, Mrs. Keller."

"Oh, please call me Hettie." She tried to be calm, but I could tell she was nervous. She was fidgeting with the curls behind her ear and she blurted out, "How do you like my hair? I had a perm this morning for the occasion of our meeting."

I told her how pretty she looked and she blushed. "Come on back and I'll show you my room." She stood up and I handed her the cane. I held out my left elbow so she could place her right hand on my arm, and we walked together down the corridor.

"How do you know how to lead a blind person?"

"They taught me at the Center for the Visually Impaired."

She squeezed my arm as if she approved. "They did a good job," she said. "You're doing it just right. My room is straight ahead at the end of the hall." She stopped suddenly and I thought something was wrong. She raised her face toward mine and said, "You'll be the first gentleman I've had in my room since I've been here."

"Who says I'm a gentleman?"

She laughed. "You sound like my kind of man."

When we reached the bedroom, I saw piles of books with black cardboard covers stacked along every wall. Braille books are three times the size of a regular book. The musty smell of old paper filled the room. Two beige wingchairs sat beside her bed along with a nightstand. On the wall opposite her bed stood a mahogany dresser with more books stacked on top. She had a small bathroom with a sink, toilet and shower. There was a closet next to the dresser.

I asked, "How long have you had these books?"

"There's no telling," she answered. "Do you like to read? Will you read a book with me?"

"I love to read and we can read together. Where do you get these Braille books?"

"There's a library for the blind in town. Why don't you get a book from your library and then get me the same one in Braille, and we could read page for page? You read one page and then I read the next. But, right now I'm hungry. Did you bring the fried chicken like you promised?"

"Yes, but I left it in the kitchen. Here, let me help you into your chair and I'll be back with the food." I returned with boxes from Kentucky Fried Chicken and pulled the other chair up close to hers. She told me on the phone that she wanted fried chicken drumsticks, mashed potatoes with gravy, macaroni and cheese, and a surprise for dessert. I left two drumsticks in the box and set it on her lap. She ate the chicken by herself and I spoon-fed her everything else. Later that afternoon, when I visited with Carol, I asked her whether she usually helped Hettie eat. She told me Hettie was capable of eating all foods by herself and seldom spilled anything at the community table. She loved the attention of my feeding her so I continued it every time we ate together.

When we finished lunch Hettie asked, "Did you bring a dessert?"

"Yes, ma'am." I reached for the plastic container of apple pie and removed the lid.

"Oh boy, I love apple pie!" Hettie said.

I was shocked, "How did you know?"

"I could smell it. When you lose your eyesight all of your other senses are sharpened."

"How?"

Hettie leaned back in her chair, raised her chin and said, "You learn to pay attention to your other senses and therefore you use them more. It's a process of adjusting."

After we finished the meal I asked her, "How did you like our first lunch together?"

"Oh, I thought it was terrific, but all this cholesterol is going to kill me someday."

I laughed. "If you don't mind me asking, how old are you, Hettie?"

"Never ask a woman her age."

"Oh, I'm sorry."

"I was just kidding. I'll be ninety-four-years old on the 29th day of July. What are you going to get me for my birthday?"

That question surprised me, and I almost laughed out loud. "I'll get you anything you want. Just name it."

She thought for a few seconds and said, "I want a locket and I want you to put your picture in it."

"OK, I'll bring you a locket with my picture." But I wondered why she'd want a photograph she couldn't see.

Hettie said, "When is your birthday? And how old are you?"

"Mine is just a few days past yours. I'll be fifty-five on the third day of August.

She sprang to her feet. "Can we have a party? Can we have a party?"

Her energy shocked me. "Of course we can," I said. "What's your favorite cake?"

"Coconut!"

"Then coconut it will be."

She smiled and sat in her chair. I picked up one of the books stacked along the wall and said, "I'd love to see how you read Braille."

"I'd be happy to oblige. Please set a book in my lap."

I gave her the book and she opened the cover and skimmed her fingers across the first page. "Ah, a great story – One Hundred Years of Solitude by Marquez."

"I like your taste in books already."

"Thank you."

The pages were about eighteen inches square and she slid both of her index fingers side by side across the raised bumps from left to right. When she reached the end of each line she moved her left index finger to the beginning of the line below, dropped her right index finger down next to it and moved them both across the bumps. She told me the left finger gave her clarification of anything she might have missed with the right finger.

I watched in astonishment as she read Braille as fast as I read print. "May I see what it feels like?"

"Sure, go right ahead."

I reached over with my fingers and closed my eyes as I skimmed them across the bumps. "Gosh, this seems impossible, and I thought learning the Russian language was hard."

Hettie said, "It's no harder for me than reading by sight is for you. I learned Braille at an early age. Later, I taught blind children how to read. What do you do for a living?"

"I lease and sell office buildings in Atlanta."

"That sounds exciting. Do you like your work?"

"I'm crazy about it. The business is competitive and rewarding. I travel all over the country selling Atlanta to corporate America."

Hettie said, "I want to hear more about your job."

"You will. I promise. There are lots of exciting stories to tell you, but for now please tell me about your childhood and how you learned Braille."

She told me about her birth in Northeast Georgia in Hart County near the town of Elberton. She called it "my miracle of survival." Her sharecropper mother, holding a hoe, slumped over in labor pains and fell screaming into the black dirt of a north Georgia cotton field. Hettie's father yelled for help. A neighbor came high stepping over the summer cotton, bringing with him a pail of water, a tattered sheet and a mumbled prayer. Hettie was born on that sheet in July of 1899 as her mother clutched the hoe and stared at a red-tailed hawk circling above in a cloudless blue sky. She was three months premature and weighed less than two pounds. Four months later both of her eyes became infected and she lost her sight.

"Mother told me that story many times," she said. "My grandmother, who was full-blooded Cherokee, told mother it was a sign of good luck to be born under a red-tailed hawk."

Hettie Keller surprised and impressed me with that remark. She never said a word about the bad luck of losing her sight.

She told me about her education. "Mom and Dad kept talking about how smart I was and they told me about the Georgia School for the Blind in Macon. They encouraged me to go to school. Of course, that meant that I had to leave home at seven-years old."

"From your house to Macon is over two-hundred miles. How did you get there?"

"You know, I remember that day as if it were yesterday."

She told me her dad hitched up the two-mule wagon, the one they used to haul cotton and they left their home in Hart County early one morning. It was a two-day ride to the train station in Toccoa. On the first night, they all slept in the back of the wagon alongside a rural dirt road. Her mother packed food for her trip and put it in a burlap sack. It contained clothes, sandwiches, apples and a jar of lemonade.

.

"They helped me on the train, and walked me back to my seat. I knew I wouldn't be with them again until school was out the next summer."

"And it was September when you left home?"

"Yes, and I remember how alone and petrified I felt when my parents got off of the train."

"You must have been scared to death."

"Was I ever? Remember that I had never been anywhere by myself. I was sitting there holding onto my sack and the sound of clickety, clickety, click started singing in my ears. It was a soothing sound and it reminded me of the fiddle Daddy used to play. I started humming to the tune of the wheels rolling on the rails. A man the passengers called 'Conductor' came up to me and said, 'Riding a train is fun. Are you having a good time?' I told him I liked the sound of the wheels, but I missed my mom and dad. He sat next to me and told me about his seven-year-old daughter."

She paused and I asked her, "How did you like school?"

"I loved it. Our farm was isolated, I never had a friend until I went to school and they assigned a girl named Alice to room with me. We were alike in so many ways. Her parents were farmers in South Carolina and she was away from home for the first time too. We studied together and many times we fell asleep talking to each other. Making friends with her helped me overcome the loneliness of missing my parents. She had a strange Southern accent. Have you heard them speak?"

"Yes, I lived in Charleston when I was in the third and fourth grade. Their accent can be explained with this sentence – 'there's a moose in the hoose, let him oot.' "

She laughed and said, "There's a mouse in the house let him out."

"What kind of games did you and Alice play?"

"We played 'dress up' and walked around the campus in each other's clothes."

"Were you friends for a long time?"

"Yes, for several years until she went back home. I don't know if Alice is still alive, but the thought of her is with me often. Our friendship was one of the best things that ever happened to me. It gave me confidence to know that other people liked me beside my parents. Confidence is so important in the development of a person. Don't you think?"

"I agree. It's impossible to measure the lasting value of confidence. Your parent's faith in you and your abilities made a difference in your life."

"I'll say. They were always supportive and Momma loved for me to read to her while swinging on the front porch after we moved to Cabbagetown in Atlanta."

"When did your parents move from the farm in Hart County?"

"I believe it was 1911 when we came here."

"Where did your father work?"

"The Fulton Cotton Mill – he walked to work from our home."

After Hettie finished the school year in Macon, she came back home and picked cotton during the summer. She completed her elementary and high school years and later she studied at the Perkins Institute for the Blind in Massachusetts. In 1927 she completed "The Harvard Course" taught by Perkins and the Harvard Graduate School of Education.

"Isn't Perkins where Helen Keller and Annie Sullivan went to school?"

"Yes, it is one of the most renowned schools for the blind in the world."

"Do you have any living relatives, Hettie?"

"No, my husband, Joe, was the last to go."

Now I understood why the Center for the Visually Impaired had sent me to see her. There are several jobs a volunteer can do for the blind: record books for listeners, work at the center's office on Peachtree Street, or visit a blind person. I chose to be what the center called a "Friendly Visitor."

The man who interviewed me asked, "Is there anyone in particular you would like to visit?"

I replied, "Why don't you send me to someone who needs a friend the most?"

He said, "That would be Hettie Keller."

"Why?"

"She is the most independent person I have ever known. She is ninety-three years old and we recently convinced her to move from her house into a small nursing home. People were stealing from her during the day and she was no longer safe. She hates the nursing home. We've sent four people to see her and they all came back and said, 'No thanks.' "

"So, you're feeding me to the lion."

"You told me you had good people skills, but the decision is yours."

I paused and thought about my favorite uncle who lost his sight in his later years because of diabetes. I was ten-years-old and I remembered leading him around the yard of his home. He was always grateful and gave me Juicy Fruit for helping him.

"Okay, I'll see her. How long has she been blind?"

"She lost her sight a few months after she was born."

"Is she lucid?"

"She's sharp. Maybe, it's all the reading she does. Someone told me the other day that Mrs. Keller had read a book a week for sixty years."

"That's impressive. What's the best way to get in touch with her?"

"She has a phone in her room. I'll give you the number."

The drive from Atlanta to Cartersville can take forty-five minutes to three hours. Traffic is brutal on I-75. It gave me time to think about the best way to approach Mrs. Keller. My entire business career had been in sales. I always tried to see the CEO, and their gatekeepers were professionals. One word stood out in my thought process - chocolate. I called her later that afternoon.

She answered in a gruff voice, "Hello!"

"Mrs. Keller, my name is Arnold Heflin and I'm going to be your new Friendly Visitor."

Silence.

I said, "What's your favorite candy?"

She mumbled, "Chocolate."

"What kind of chocolate?"

Her voice mellowed a bit, "I love the Hershey Bar."

"With or without almonds?"

"Just the plain."

"You have a bad reputation for running off volunteers. I'm sending you a dozen Hershey Bars tomorrow."

Her response was clear and pleasant, "Why thank you very much."

She was on her best behavior during our first visit. I could tell she wanted to make a good impression on me. She engaged me in conversation and said, "Tell me a story about your childhood. Something funny."

"Well, like your life, my tale must begin with my parents, especially my mother. All I ever wanted to do when I was growing up in Birmingham, Alabama, was play ball and please my momma. She was Irish in the truest sense of the word. She had coal black eyes that sparkled and danced a second before she smiled. She was the greatest mom who ever lived and I've missed her every day since her death."

Hettie said, "When did you lose her?"

"June 8, 1981 at 5:22 p.m."

"Six years after Joe. And what year was she born?"

"1908."

"So, I'm nine years older than your mother, please continue."

"I remember the sweet scent of Mom's perfume and the warm comfort of her arms around me. We rocked back and forth in her favorite chair and she'd recite: 'May the road rise to meet you. May the wind be always at your back. May the sun shine warm upon your face, the rain fall soft upon your fields, and until we meet again may God hold you in the palm of His hand."

"Ah, yes, the Irish Prayer," Hettie said. "I remember it well."

"Mother was short in stature, but a giant in moral character. I seldom saw her frown at me but when she did it was the thought of disappointing her that made me feel bad. The worst look I ever got from her happened when I was ten-years-old. I was in the fifth grade at St. Clements and I bought my first yo-yo, a Duncan. The yo-yo manufacturers hired Hawaiians to come to the grammar schools and teach kids how to do tricks like Walk the Dog, Rock the Cradle, Around the World, and Loop the Loop."

"Arnold, that's as mysterious to me as Braille is to you. I'm familiar with a yo-yo. Once, someone slipped the string around my finger and I let it fall out of my hand. But those tricks with such strange names, I've never heard of them. What was your favorite?"

"Loop the Loop. I'll try and describe it for you. You cup the yo-yo with the palm of your hand on top of it and throw it straight out from your waist. When it reaches the end of the string, it comes zooming back in your direction and you lower your hand and let the yo-yo pass over it before you whirl it out again. The kids who were real good could do four to five hundred Loop the Loops. I was excellent. I had been practicing to enter a citywide yo-yo contest downtown at the Alabama Theater.

"For people living in Alabama during the 1940s this theater was Birmingham's Carnegie Hall. It was a grand old place with an organist and a huge balcony. It held two thousand people and it would be packed on the day of the contest because the first prize was a brand new bicycle. In 1948 a new bike was on the top of my wish list. On competition day, there were hundreds of kids with yo-yos in their pockets. The contest required that you perform five basic tricks, and the person who did the most Loop the Loops won the bicycle. Hettie, I carried that yo-yo with me everywhere I went. I placed it under my pillow every night."

She laughed.

"It was during Lent and Mom took my younger brother, my sister and me to church every time the doors opened. We went there every Friday evening for the Stations of the Cross. After the service, we went to the rectory. Older ladies sat behind a portable table selling holy articles like rosaries, medals and prayer books. After buying a holy article, usually you have it blessed by a priest. The blessing is short and simple. He makes the sign of the cross over it with his hand and says, 'In the name of the Father, the Son, and the Holy Spirit.' I was waiting for my mom and pulled the yo-yo out of my pocket and began to practice Loop the

Loops. Suddenly a woman came out of nowhere, and while practicing I knocked her large purple hat off with my yo-yo."

Hettie laughed, "That's funny."

"The lady screamed and Mother came over to me and said, 'Put that yo-yo in your pocket and leave it there. Go and apologize to Mrs. Simpson.' I did what I was told and sat down. I began to think about the new bicycle I'd be riding in two weeks.

"It was a good night for holy articles, because there was a long line in front of Father Kennan. I stood in it just to pass the time and in a few minutes I heard the priest say, 'Arnold, do you have something you want me to bless?'

"I said, 'Yes, Father, please bless this.' Father Kennan was not looking at me when I reached into my pocket and pulled out my yo-yo. I figured with his blessing my chances of riding a new bike would be almost guaranteed. I held the yo-yo in my hand and without looking down the priest made the sign of the cross over it. Just as I was about to put it back into my pocket, he shouted, 'YOU HAD ME BLESS A YO-YO! YOU HAVE COMMITTED A SACRILEGE!' I had no idea what a sacrilege was, but I knew I'd never seen one."

Hettie was shaking with laughter. "Please hand me a Kleenex from my night stand." She dabbed her eyes. "You were in real trouble then. Weren't you?"

"Yes, ma'am I was. Mother rushed over to me and said, 'I told you to keep that yo-yo in your pocket.' Oh, the look she gave me hurt, but the real pain came later when we got home. Mom was not the administrator of punishment. I never asked her about it, but she and my father must have had an agreement that she would do the scolding and he would do the spanking. She told him about Father Kennan blessing the yo-yo. I thought I saw a gleam in his eye, but he said, 'Son, follow me to the basement.'

"I can count on one hand the number of spankings I've had in my life. Dad had a razor strap that was a heavy piece of leather about two feet long and four inches wide. I remember walking behind him down the basement steps; I stared at the dark strap in his right hand. It was scary. When we reached the bottom, he said, 'Take your pants down and turn around.' I took a deep breath. The basement had an odor of unpleasantness. Before I dropped my pants he said, 'Son, this is going to hurt me worse than it will you.'

"Why do it then?"

Hettie chuckled.

"He said, 'I don't have a choice. Your mother said you committed a sacrilege.'

"What is a sacrilege, Dad?"

"I don't know."

"My dad was not Catholic and the only time he went to church was on Easter or Christmas. He was a good father, and I know for a fact this was one spanking he regretted. Years later I asked him whether he remembered it and he told me it had been difficult for him not to laugh when my mother had told him about the blessing of the yo-yo.

"In the basement, he said, 'When I spank you, I want you to cry.'

"I answered, 'Crying is for sissies.'

"Dad said, 'I'll stop when you cry. Bend over.'

"Whap! I didn't cry. Whap! I didn't cry again. Whap! Whap! Whap! The only sound came from the strap. The basement door opened and I saw Mother at the top of the stairs. Dad threw the strap on the floor and yelled, 'Damn it, Millie. If you want him spanked you can come down here and finish it!' When he walked upstairs I pulled my pants up and snatched the yo-yo out of my pocket and began to do some Loop the Loops. My fanny hurt, but I knew I was going to win that bike now that my yo-yo was blessed. Sacrilege or no sacrilege."

Hettie said, "I sure hope you won the contest."

"That's best part of the story," I told her. "The yo-yo competition was held two weeks later on a Saturday afternoon before a movie. The Alabama Theater was packed. There were eighty-seven contestants who performed all of the basic tricks, and I drew number "86" which was an advantage. That meant when I walked up on the stage I knew how many Loop the Loops I'd have to beat. The boy who drew number "87" went to my school and I knew I could beat him. When my turn came, the highest number of Loop the Loops were four-hundred-nine. That blessed yo-yo was singing on the string for me and when I reached three hundred everyone in the audience began to count out loud. When the total reached three-hundred-ninety, I could feel the wind blowing my hair as I flew down hills on the new red Schwinn. The crowd counted in unison: '396, 397, 398,' and suddenly a loud groan. The yo-yo string broke on three-hundred-ninety-nine; my Duncan sailed out into the audience. As I trudged off the stage I thought, 'I should have had Father Kennan bless that package of strings, too.' "

We laughed as our first visit came to an end. Carol came in and said, "Mrs. Keller, what were you laughing about so much?"

"Loop the Loops."

Carol jerked her head around and looked at Mrs. Keller. "Say what?"

Hettie said, "I'll tell you the story later." We said our goodbyes and I walked down the corridor with Carol.

Carol said, "What do you think about her?"

"She's nothing like I expected. She's got a good attitude once you get to know her. She's lonely. What happened with the previous visitors?"

"She said they all treated her like a child. This woman is chocked full of independence and she will not take nonsense from anyone."

I said, "She's so smart and pleasant. I don't understand."

"I don't either. Please stop and visit with me in the kitchen."

"I will. How many women do you have here besides Hettie?"

"There are five others, but Mrs. Keller is the only blind person we have."

We sat on barstools next to the counter and talked for thirty minutes. Carol told me she felt like Hettie came there hoping to die. The confinement of the nursing home was too much for her. Her appetite had dropped. I told Carol that she ate everything on her plate this afternoon. Carol begged me to continue to see her. She said, "I have not heard laughter from her since she arrived two months ago."

"She did laugh a lot this afternoon. I enjoyed it too and I'll be back next Saturday."

Carol said, "Do you mind if I call you, Arnie?"

"Not at all. That was my high school nickname."

"I'll see you next Saturday, Arnie."

CHAPTER TWO

Hettie called me on a Wednesday evening several months after we met. "I hate to bother you at home, but I need a favor."

"How can I help you?"

"I fell yesterday and hurt my shoulder. Can you take me to the doctor tomorrow?"

"Yes, I'm sorry to hear about your fall. How are you feeling?"

"My shoulder hurts, but not too bad."

"What time is your appointment?"

I heard her talking to Carol and after a short pause she said, "Ten in the morning."

"OK," I said, "I will pick you up at 9:30 and I'll have a wheelchair with me." Carol told me earlier that Hettie did fine walking short distances, but suggested if I ever took her out of the home, she'd do better in a wheelchair.

Driving into the city the next day, I reflected on my relationship with Hettie. The first few weeks were difficult. She took the word "independent" to a higher level. We both were strong willed and it created conflict. We had a hard time selecting the books we read on Saturday. She read only fiction and I loved nonfiction. Several times I suggested something to eat other than fried chicken. She shook her head like a two-year-old child.

She had a good mind and her ability to recall events in her early years was remarkable. Her maternal grandmother was a Cherokee shaman and Hettie inherited her quality of spirit. Sometimes, she seemed to possess a sixth sense. She knew things that blind people should have never known. Maybe it was her love for knowledge and reading. She had read a book a week for sixty years. When she first told me that, I found it hard to believe, but on one of my visits to the Library for the Blind in Atlanta, I asked them how long they had been in the city. They told me the library opened in the early 1930s. The books were mailed free to their customers and she confirmed that Hettie Keller was one of their longest and most frequent patrons.

Her parents were brilliant in the lessons they taught her. One day when she was five-years-old, the three of them were sitting on the bank of the creek at the rear of the sixty acres they farmed. They had taken a break from the tedious work of hoeing the cotton during a hot summer day. They had their shoes off and were cooling their feet in the creek. A cottonmouth water moccasin bit Hettie in the back of the ankle. The nickname for the cottonmouth is "trap jaw" because their jaws can close shut in an instant. Hettie screamed. Her father grabbed the tail of snake and jerked it off of her and then he broke its neck with a vicious snap. He lifted her in his arms and carried her to the house. Her mother went straight to the woods looking for a particular kind of root. Shamans used roots and leaves to cure snakebites, fevers, headaches, coughs and toothaches.

Her mother boiled the root and applied the potion. Hettie's leg was swollen for a few days and she suffered from pain and nausea. Her dad took her back to the creek after she healed. He asked her to take her shoes off and put her feet in the water and he told her that he would never let a snake bite her again. He carried a sturdy stick with him every time they relaxed at the creek. He gave her a lesson in courage and trust which lasted her entire life. When she told me the story, I wondered how her dad had the foresight to know a blind person must have those two virtues to thrive. Hettie was the epitome of courage and her dad had planted the seed. I thought about that story for weeks and I could not get it out of my mind. I asked Hettie if she realized how much influence her parents had on her. She told me she did. She never said an unkind word about her parents or husband. She made fun of Mrs. Weldon's snoring in the room next to her and accused Carol of stealing her Hershey Bars, but she never said a bad word about her family.

She told me the first few years of her life were spent helping her mom and dad with the cotton. They did not have a radio but her dad played the fiddle and they sang together in the evening. Her mother read to her almost every night while they sat in a rocking chair by the fireplace.

The more I saw her the more she mellowed and she had a good sense of humor. We laughed together quite often on each visit. I had several close relationships with women since my divorce and there comes a time in each where the comfort zone kicks in and you can relax and be yourself. Hettie and I were comfortable with each other now and I looked forward to seeing her and Carol on Saturdays.

I pulled in the driveway of the home a few minutes early and Carol was outside watering a multicolored bed of zinnias. She said, "What's up, Arnie? Thank you for coming to take Hettie to the doctor this morning. I hope she didn't break anything when she fell."

" Me too. How's she doing"?

"She's okay, but I think it will be good to have a doctor x-ray her shoulder. Arnie, how do you stay so fit?"

"I walk four miles a day, five days a week and I never eat anything but fruit after 8 p.m."

"Get out of here. How can you be so disciplined?"

"My dad taught me a good lesson that has always stayed with me. He told me if you do something for twenty-one consecutive days it will become a habit."

"If I lost thirty pounds, I might find me a man. I'm going to be thirty-three in August and I do not want to spend the rest of my life alone. Being this tall and overweight is a bad combination when it comes to finding a beau."

I reached over and grabbed her hand, "You are a beautiful woman and you have plenty of time to find a man."

"Do you have a girlfriend?"

"Not now, but I don't worry about it. The best way to find a mate is to let them find you."

"You are a handsome dude. I can see why you never have a problem in meeting women. Where do you meet most of them?"

"In a grocery store."

"Are you serious? Why would it happen in a grocery store?"

"I don't have an answer, but let me ask you what day of the week do you do your shopping?"

"I'm off on Wednesdays and Sundays and that's when I buy groceries."

"Why don't you shop on Friday evening around seven p.m.? Go home after work and fix yourself up like you were going on a date to the Braves game. Now, the key to the success of this operation begins with the basket selection. Get the big cart even though you are buying only a few items. Here's what you place in the cart - a quart of milk."

"Why?"

"Because you are wholesome and healthy."

"Get you a can of dog food."

"How can that help me meet a man?"

"Most men love dogs. Get you a pint of chocolate ice cream."

"Are you trying to fatten me up? Why ice cream? Why chocolate?"

"Men like chocolate and they love women who buy chocolate ice cream. Also, get you an instant meal. It's best to get Chicken Parmesan."

"How do you know all this?"

I reached into my pocket and pulled out a small notebook and began flipping through the pages. Carol didn't know I was playing with her and I could feel the intensity of her stare. I stopped and stared at a page and said, "Let's see. Right here it says that

Chicken Parmesan works forty-four percent of the time." When I looked at Carol she was smiling and shaking her head.

"Arnie, either you are playing with me or you are flat out crazy."

I laughed, closed the notebook and put it in my pocket. "Love lesson number one is over for the day, but the Parmesan does work."

I brought a wheelchair from the local hospital in Cartersville and I rolled it into Hettie's room and picked her up for our first trip outside the home. After I helped her into the car, I fastened her seatbelt and started the engine. I looked over at her and said, "Do you want to make a run for it?"

She laughed and said, "My shoulder just got better. Let's go to Panama City, Florida where the beaches are covered with fluffy sand."

"So you've been to Panama City?"

"Yes, Joe and I drove there with some friends on our tenth wedding anniversary. We walked along the beach barefooted and the fine sand squished between my toes. It was the only time in my life that I have ever been to the beach. The waves frightened my guide dog, Sarge. When they came in he wanted to run away from them. Joe and I took off our shoes and walked along the beach. It was the greatest time for us."

I thought it was too bad she couldn't see where they were walking because the white sand and the blue-green water give Panama City one of the most scenic beaches in the world.

"I'd love to hear more about your guide dogs someday. Did you and Joe both have dogs?"

"No, just me. Do you like dogs?"

"I love them."

"I had guide dogs for fifty years and I'm looking forward to telling you about them, but we'll save that for another time. Now tell me, have you ever been to Panama City?"

"Many times. That place has changed so much since you were there in 1948. There are high-rise condominiums all along the beach."

"What's a high-rise condominium?"

Hettie was so well read that I talked to her as if she had sight all of her life. "Well, a condominium is where people live. It's like an apartment building except you own your unit. They're called condos."

"I understand, but explain high-rise to me."

"High-rise means the building is tall – say twenty stories or higher."

"What do you mean by stories?"

I thought, "How do I explain this one?"

She said, "Am I asking too many questions?"

"Not at all. A story of a building is about ten feet high."

She was facing in my direction while I kept my eyes on I-85. Hettie said, "So, if one story is ten feet, a twenty-story condominium is two-hundred feet tall. Wow."

We entered the Midtown section of Atlanta where her doctor was located on 10th Street. I said, "There are office buildings near us that are six-hundred feet tall. These are the kind of buildings I sell and lease."

"I don't know how you stand the elevator rides every day. My stomach always feels like it's dropping to my knees when the elevator goes up. Did you study real estate in college?"

"No, I majored in Journalism and English."

"Where did you go to school?"

"I graduated from Auburn University in 1961."

"When did you come to Atlanta?"

"I moved here in 1966."

We were driving by Piedmont Park, one-hundred-ninety acres of gardens, lakes, trees and wide-open green spaces located in the heart of the city. I looked out the window and saw autumn leaves falling. A young man and a boy around six years of age were tossing a football back and forth. It reminded me of my dad and an earlier time in my life. "Hettie, would you like to hear a story about my childhood?"

"You mean one about ten feet tall?"

I laughed. "You don't miss a thing do you?"

She smiled. "I'd love to hear your story."

"The University of Alabama had great football teams during the 1940s and the star tailback lived on the same street in Birmingham that I did as a child. During the summer months, I sat on the front porch steps waiting for him to walk by with a football in his hand. He always threw me a pass. In the fall of 1943, I was five-years-old and I wrote to Santa Claus asking him for one present – a football. Our county's war effort was at its peak then and there was a shortage of rubber and leather; the two things needed to make a football.

"On Christmas morning I ran into the living room only to find a letter from Santa. 'Dear Arnold, thanks for the milk and cookies. The sugar cookies were yummy. I'm sorry I could not bring your football. All of my leather and rubber are being used to make boots for our soldiers. As soon as my elves can make footballs again, I'll fly to Birmingham with my reindeer and bring your ball. Remember to brush your teeth everyday."

"Hettie said, "You sure can tell your parents wrote that note."

I laughed and continued, "Every morning after Christmas I ran into the living room to see if the football was there. When I did not see it, I dropped my head and shuffled into the bathroom to brush my teeth. The sight of his son being disappointed every morning became too much for my dad. He moved from the living room to the kitchen to drink his coffee. My father became a football detective. He asked everyone he met if they knew where he could find a football.

"In June of 1944, I hustled into the living room once again. There on the hardwood floor in the middle of the room sat my football with a red bow on top. I dove on it like I was recovering a fumble. That morning dad was sitting in the living room with a big grin on his face. I asked him, 'Do you want to play catch?' He put his arm around my shoulder and held his coffee cup in his other hand. With the ball cradled in my arm, we walked out to the back yard.

"The scent of honeysuckle was everywhere. The morning dew felt cool on my bare feet. Dad set his cup on the back steps and said, 'Run out for a pass.' I raced toward the chicken coop in the far corner of the yard and he tossed the ball high into the air. It was way over my head. I ran harder. As the ball fell to the ground I dove with my arms outstretched. A split second before I skimmed across the wet grass, the ball dropped into to my hands."

"Dad yelled, 'Wow! What a catch!'"

Hettie said, "I don't know a lot about football. How long did you play?"

"All the way into college until I tore up my knee."

We pulled into the doctor's parking lot and I turned off the engine. "We're here, Hettie."

She said, "Before we go in, tell me about your injury and how it happened. I can tell from the sound of your voice how much it disappointed you."

I said, "We don't have time now. Let me get you inside and I'll tell you on the way home."

"Don't forget."

I removed her wheelchair from the trunk and helped her into it. As I pushed her along, I said, "This building is not a high-rise. It's about eight or nine stories so I call it a mid-rise building."

Hettie said, "Hey, as fast as I'm learning real estate, I'll be selling office buildings before you know it. Do you need an assistant?"

"Yes, I do, but do you think your stomach can handle the elevators?"

"Oh, I forgot about that. On second thought, I have too many books to read."

We got on the elevator and I grinned when I saw Hettie's mouth drop as it moved upward. I wheeled her into the reception room to find forty people waiting for several doctors. Most of them were thumbing through old magazines. The silence of the room had a presence of its own. Hettie and I sat next to each other in quiet contemplation and then she asked me in a voice loud enough to be heard by all, "Arnold, do you think they are going to operate on my shoulder?"

I've always had a good sense of timing when it comes to humor. I paused for a few seconds before answering her question. I waited until most of the people had looked up from their magazines and in our direction. Then I replied, "That all depends on whether you want to continue your trapeze work." Hettie laughed so hard she leaned forward and her body began to slide out of the wheelchair. I jumped up and lifted her back into place.

We left the doctor's office an hour later. Her shoulder had a slight strain and she would recover with no problem.

"Are you hungry, Hettie? Let's have our first meal out together."

She clapped her hands. "Can we go to Morrison's?"

"The cafeteria? Of course, we can."

She turned toward me. "They have the greatest desserts in the world."

I stepped on the gas pedal and the car lurched forward. "Okay, let's hurry up."

We pulled up outside Morrison's and I got her in the wheelchair. We entered the cafeteria at the noon rush hour and it took us awhile to get through the serving line. We talked about food the whole time we waited. When we reached the counter, I described the salads to Hettie, and she chose carrot and raisin. The desserts were next, before the entrees. There were many choices and I decided to have some fun with her keen sense of smell. I stepped around in front of her and said, "Let's play a game."

"I love games. What are we going to play?"

"I'm going to pick out a dessert and hold it in front of you. Then you try and tell me what it is." I picked up a plate of chocolate pie and said, "What is it?"

She took a deep breath. "You started with an easy one. Chocolate pie."

"You got that right. You're one out of one."

Next, I grabbed a bowl of peach cobbler. "What's this?"

She sat up higher in the wheelchair and said, "Peach cobbler."

"Right again."

Everyone in front of us continued to move down the serving line and the people behind us came to a halt. Next, I picked up strawberry shortcake. "Tell me what this is?"

"Strawberry shortcake with pound cake and not biscuits."

"Very good," I answered. "I'm going to make the next one harder."

Behind us in line, a tall man with a gruff voice said, "What's the hold-up?"

I answered him, "I have an elderly person with me and we'll be moving along in a minute."

He said, "I'm sorry. Take your time."

I searched for something I thought might have a chance to fool her. I picked out a piece of lemon icebox pie and placed it in front of her. "OK, what's this?"

Hettie took about three whiffs and said, "Lemon pie."

"That's right, but tell me if it is lemon meringue or lemon icebox?"

She smiled, "That's easy. It's lemon ice box."

A few of the people behind us clapped for Hettie. The employees behind the serving line moved down in our direction and they were watching our game.

Hettie was inspired by the sound of applause. "Try another one," she said.

I picked up a dish of butterscotch pudding. "What do we have here?"

She didn't hesitate. "Butterscotch pudding."

The employees cheered her on, "Way to go."

The people standing behind us moved in closer so they could see. People cheered and clapped. Hettie's face was flush with a tint of pink. She loved the attention of the crowd. Later, I learned she had performed on stage in a musical production at the Fox Theater on Atlanta's Peachtree Street. Maybe the applause brought back some of those good memories.

She said, "Go ahead. Try some more."

We went through pound cake, pumpkin pie, raspberries, blackberries, key lime pie and others. On each answer the crowd roared with approval. From the noise in the cafeteria line you would have thought Michael Jordan had made a last-second jump shot to win the game. I saved her favorite dessert for last and placed the coconut cake on her tray. We moved down the line as everyone clapped. She had a big smile.

When we finished lunch and got in the car she said, "That was the best meal I've ever had."

I replied, "I think I'm too full to drive to Panama City. Maybe we'll do that another time."

She laughed.

When we returned to the home, I saw a cardinal in a maple tree next to the driveway. I asked Hettie, "Have you ever listened to birds?"

"Yes, I have. They always bring cheer." She smiled and said, "I love the mockingbird's song. You can never tell where the bird is going with its tune. It'll sing for a half an hour or longer. As a young girl, I remember sitting next to our house in the high grass of spring and listening to the tune of the mockingbird." Then she frowned.

"What's wrong?" I asked.

She sighed, "I don't think, I'll ever hear that song again."

"Well, you never can tell. Did you ever think you'd receive an ovation in Morrison's?"

She laughed. "Absolutely not. Being around you, I've learned a day can be full of surprises. There is no telling what comes next with you. You sure have brought a lot of joy into my life."

I said, "You're fun to be with too. Now, we'd better get inside so you can get your afternoon nap." We walked into the home and she gave Carol a report from the doctor. Then we headed to Hettie's room. I fluffed the pillow and helped her onto her bed. I pulled the blue-and-white afghan over her legs, sat on the edge of the bed and held her hand.

She said, "You did something special for me today. The next time you come to see me; I'm going to do something special for you."

I leaned down and kissed her on the cheek for the first time as she nodded off to sleep.

On the way home, I thought, "She wanted to know more about my football injury, but I'm glad I forgot to mention it again." It was a freak accident that ripped apart the medial collateral ligament. It happened on a practice field in front of a couple hundred people. All those dreams of playing big-time college football were gone in a second.

Compared with Hettie's childhood illness, mine now seemed insignificant. It had been hard for me to let go of that incident. Every time I watched football on television and someone hurt his knee, I thought of those minutes and later hours in agony. But what really hurt was the loss of my athletic career. It was over in a second. Today I looked at it in a different way. How petty my knee injury seemed compared with Hettie Keller's loss of sight when she was four months old.

I thought about her parting words, "You did something special for me today. The next time you come to see me I'm going to do something special for you."

CHAPTER THREE

Several times during the week I thought about what Hettie had said and I was full of anxiety as I drove into Atlanta to see her. We both were hungry and we devoured our lunch. She leaned her head against the back of the chair and I stood and stretched for a moment. I sat down and she said, "What do we have for dessert?"

"You tell me Scent Master." I removed two brownies from a sack.

"We got us some brownies today," she said.

I gave her one. She smiled and took a bite and said, "Brownies always remind me of Joe Keller, I'd fix them for him while he was at work. When he opened the front door he always said, 'Did my sweetheart make me some brownies today?' Let me tell you a funny story about Joe Keller and a game we used to play."

"I'd love to hear it."

She leaned back in her chair and smiled. I don't think she ever mentioned Joe's name without a pleasant look on her face. She adored him.

"Joe sold brooms for a living and he worked hard. He'd leave in the morning with about a dozen brooms in his arms and then he'd come home for lunch. After we ate and spent a few minutes talking, he left for the afternoon with his arms full of brooms again. He came home around six o'clock. Whenever he left the house or returned, we always gave each other a hug and kiss.

"Sometimes when he came home in the evening, while we hugged, I'd sneak my hand into his pocket where he kept his change, grab a few quarters and put them in my purse. Later, when he emptied his pockets, he'd say, 'I thought I sold more brooms than this today.' He knew then that I had taken the quarters, but I always gave them back to him. We had fun together."

I asked her, "When is the last time you've been to the cemetery where Joe Keller is buried?"

"I haven't been there since the funeral in 1975." She paused and said, "Gosh, that's nineteen years ago."

"Would you like to go?"

"Yes! Will you take me?"

"Sure, we'll go one sunny spring day and I'll get some flowers for you to put on the grave."

She clapped her hands. "Can we eat our chicken outside on a blanket?"

"Yes ma'am, we'll have our picnic on a blanket in the high grass of spring."

"Will you bring more brownies when we have our picnic. Those were delicious. Now, please bring me a cup of coffee."

"Good idea. I'd love a cup too. There is something I want to talk to Carol about and it might be a few minutes or so before I return."

"Take your time, I have a good read going."

I walked into the kitchen where Carol was cleaning up after lunch. While Hettie and I ate in her room, Carol had been feeding the other women in the home.

Carol said, "I bet you're looking for some coffee."

"Yeah, and that smells like a fresh pot."

"It is. I just want you to know your visits mean everything to Mrs. Keller. You won't believe how much she talks about you. She told us about the ovation she received in the cafeteria last week."

"I really appreciate the care you give her. I'm just here one day a week."

Carol smiled and said, "Thank you, Arnie."

I said, "Hettie didn't like it at all when she first arrived, did she?"

"No, that woman was hard to live with until you came to see her. Now she's a pleasure to be around."

"Well, she had just lost her freedom, and I don't blame her for being down in the dumps."

Carol said, "Yes, freedom is precious, especially when you are as independent as Mrs. Keller. On another note, Arnie, I tried your idea at the store last night and three different men spoke to me."

"See there."

"They were good looking men too."

"How many times did you walk around the store?"

"Only once."

"Okay, your freedom may be short lived."

"How long have you been divorced?" Carol asked.

"Fifteen years and if your asking me do I love my independence, the answer is yes."

"Carol said, "That's what I'm thinking too. It is such a pleasure to do what you want to do without telling anyone. Many times I've thought about how hard that would be to give up, but I think about my elder years alone and it is not a good thought. Besides, I love children and I want to have them. I want to hold them, cuddle them and smell baby powder. That is the sweetest smell on earth."

"I love the aroma of baby powder too. Since I have two grown children and realize the difficulty of raising them in a large city full of dangerous temptations, I no longer have the desire for children and that prevented me from marrying someone a few years ago."

Carol was standing behind the counter in the kitchen and she walked over and placed her hand on top of mine. "Thank you for taking your time to spend with me. Leaving the grocery store last night, I had a warm feeling when I thought of you and your cart advice. Let me get some coffee for you and Hettie."

I carried our coffee back to Hettie's room and sat down.

She said, "Do you remember last week when I said I was going to do something special for you?"

"I remember, but I hope you didn't bake me a cake because I'm too stuffed to eat it."

She laughed. "Didn't you tell me you're fifty-five, Arnold?"

"Yes."

"You're just a young pup. I'll be ninety-five. If you live as long as I have, you have most of your adult life ahead of you."

That remark about having "most of your adult life ahead of you" really got me thinking. I had a few friends my age that thought their best years were behind them. Based on what I had seen and heard from Hettie Keller, it did not seem to be true.

"You have made such a difference and added so much pleasure to my life. I want to do something special for you. First, let me tell you that being blind has some distinct advantages."

"Really, like what?"

"I've never had the distractions that people with sight have. Most of my life has been spent with my own thoughts. I have distilled the best that I have learned about what brings you peace and happiness to thirty words. I'm going to share them with you." She leaned forward in her chair and said, "I have ten maxims of three words each. Do you know the definition of maxim?"

"I think so, but please tell me yours."

She said, "A maxim is a general truth, a fundamental principle, or a rule of conduct. Over the next few months, I'm going to give you my maxims and I promise you a life of peace and happiness if you practice them."

"That's a mighty big promise."

"Arnold, I guarantee you these ten maxims will change your life forever." She raised her chin like she was looking a foot above my head and said, "My first maxim is PRAYER ALWAYS WORKS. From our past talks, I know you believe in God. Is that right?"

"Absolutely."

"Then I assume you pray."

"I do."

"Do you ever ask God to give you something?"

"Yes, but the older I get the more experiences I have of my prayers going unanswered."

Hettie paused for a few seconds and raised her chin again. She used that mannerism when she wanted to make a point. She said, "Please tell me the last thing you prayed for that didn't happen?"

I paused to think, "Well, a few months ago, my son was trying to get a job in medical sales and I prayed every day for a month for him to be hired."

"I guess he didn't get the job."

"You're right."

"So you think your prayers went unanswered?"

"Yes."

She paused again. I waited for a spiritual revelation. She asked me, "Did the job provide for a company car?"

I was puzzled. "Actually, the company provided a van instead of a car. They sell large pieces of diagnostic equipment, and sometimes the sales people deliver them."

Hettie said, "Okay, let's assume for a moment that I am a mystic and I can see into the future."

"Do you want me to get you a crystal ball?"

"No, but thank you anyway." She bowed her head and said, "The year is 2014 and I see a crowded interstate with almost every car exceeding the speed limit."

I laughed and said, "It sounds to me like you're looking at Interstate 285 in Atlanta."

She continued, "It is a late Friday afternoon and a young man with wavy red hair is delivering a piece of medical equipment to a hospital. He has given his wife a break and brought along his three children. They are traveling in the eastbound lane. Also, I see a black tractor-trailer truck speeding in the westbound lane. The left front tire of the truck explodes and the tractor tears through a guardrail and is heading for the van driven by the young man. The three youngsters in the back seat are laughing and playing with each other. The truck smashes head-on into the van and all inside are killed." Hettie paused and then said, "The driver of the van was your son and the three children were your grandchildren."

I shuddered. "That's horrible! I do not want to hear any more morbid stories. Please, never do that again."

Hettie said, "I'm sorry to have told you such a dreadful story, but I wanted to make a point. God works in mysterious ways. You thought that your prayer went unheard. What may appear to you as an unanswered prayer was in fact a prayer answered. In the tragic example I gave you, God heard your prayer, but He also understood the great love you have for your son. He knew that it was far more important for you to enjoy him and your grandchildren for the rest your life. Therefore, the job was not in your best interest. He had better plans for both of you. God knows all!"

I sat across from a woman who had spent her entire life in darkness and realized she had just turned on a light switch in my mind. What she said made perfect sense. I nodded as if she could see me and said, "That is a powerful point."

She said, "There is a facet of prayer you should know about. The success of our prayers is directly in proportion to our faith. You can have a little bit of love for something or a lot of love for it. You can have a little bit of hope or a lot of hope. But, you can't have a little bit of faith. When it comes to faith, you must have a lot. Faith is all or nothing."

"You said prayer always works. Now you're telling me I must have total faith for prayer to work."

"Having faith is the essential ingredient in successful prayer," she said. "If you pray without faith, it's like trying to make lemonade without lemons. Just hold on a minute and I'll prove it to you." She turned toward the nightstand next to her bed. She lifted the large Braille book and placed it on her lap. She said, "Please let me find something for you."

She opened the book and her fingers explored the pages. I thought of how Hettie loved touching the words. As I observed her, I realized how words had a special meaning for her. She had spent her entire life caressing, reading and teaching words. I watched the expression on her face and saw the corners of her mouth rise in a slight smile at the recognition of certain words and phrases. Those raised bumps of Braille were her life. Words kept her connected. I knew she was reading the Bible, because that was the only book she always kept beside her bed.

"Here it is! Listen to this - these words are straight from the mouth of our Lord. In Mark, Chapter 11 Verse 24, He said, 'For this reason I tell you: When you pray and ask for something, believe that you have received it, and you will be given what you asked for.' That's as plain as it can be. Remember this: God knows what's best for all of us. If it's good for you and according to His will, you will receive what you asked for. If there is a better solution, God will choose it. You can't lose either way."

She closed the Bible and returned it to the nightstand. Then she wiggled her right forefinger. That meant she wanted me to bring my ear close enough to hear her whisper. I pulled my chair up closer and leaned over. She whispered, "Maxim Number One is PRAYER ALWAYS WORKS."

I took her hand and said, "Thank you, Hettie. You have given me a lot to think about."

She said, "You're welcome. Now, stop on your way home and get plenty of lemons."

We talked for a few more minutes and I helped her lie down for her nap. I held her hand for the last five minutes of our visit and then left. Closing the front door, I thought about what Hettie Keller had said to me this afternoon: "You have most of your adult life ahead of you. Prayer always works. If you pray without faith it's like trying to make lemonade without lemons."

I stopped in the front yard and turned to look back at the home. It was a converted six-bedroom house and Hettie's room was on the front next to the driveway. There appeared to be a glow coming from her room and I walked over to her window. The curtain was pulled back, and I looked at her asleep in the bed. She was holding the stuffed animals I had given her. They were two white Christmas mice with their arms wrapped around each other's necks. Both mice were dressed in red and green calico. I remember the Christmas afternoon when she felt the animals with her fingers. When she felt the big ears, she laughed and said, "Why, it's two mice joined together. These mice are just like you and me. They will always be a pair."

The evening sun was setting behind me, and the front window of the house was only a few feet from her bed. Hettie's face glowed in a halo of light. She had the most peaceful look I had ever seen.

I thought about what she said: "God works in mysterious ways." We had brought joy into the life of each other, and now she was giving me the keys to peace and happiness on earth. Something magical was beginning to happen in our relationship. I looked at her and thought, "Hettie Keller, our destiny brought us together."

I turned away from the window and saw a police car parked at the curb. The warm, magical feeling inside me cooled a bit. The blue lights on top of the car were blinking, and when the officer stepped toward me the expression on his face spelled trouble. He was 6'6" and built like Arnold Schwarzenegger. He bellowed, "What the hell are you doing? Get your hands over your head and don't move." The officer had on a dark uniform that made him appear even more menacing than his ominous voice. He stepped closer and said, "Turn around." When I turned my back toward him he jerked my arms down and snapped handcuffs on me. He spun me around like a top. He nodded to my car parked on the street. "Is that your vehicle?"

"Yes, sir, but let me explain."

"There's nothing to explain. You're going to jail. I've been watching you for two minutes while you were peeping into that window."

My initial apprehension had turned to anger. "Before you make a mistake, just knock on the door. They'll tell you who I am."

We walked to the door, the sergeant knocked and Carol opened it.

Holding onto my arm, the officer said, "I'm sorry to bother you ma'am. I found this man peeping into one of the windows here. Do you know him?"

Carol gazed at the rugged, handsome policeman for more than a few seconds. Then she looked at me. She examined me up and down and stared at my handcuffs. "Never seen him in my life," she said and slammed the door.

The officer barked, "Let's go!"

We were halfway down to his squad car and I thought, "This can't be happening."

Then from behind us I heard, "Wait! Wait!" We turned around and saw Carol standing in the doorway waving her arms and shouting, "Stop, officer. I was just kidding. The man you have there is Mr. Heflin. He's our favorite Friendly Visitor."

The officer said, "Sorry for the misunderstanding." He pulled the key from his pocket and unlocked the handcuffs.

As we walked back to the door, I said, "Carol, you almost got me arrested." She was laughing too hard to speak. The officer was puzzled and we both looked at Carol as her laughter continued. Carol said, "Seeing you with those handcuffs on was so funny. I would have loved to seen the expression on your face when I slammed the door."

We talked for a few minutes and I got in my car and drove away. I looked in my rearview mirror and smiled when I saw Carol and the policeman still laughing. He had his hat off and was holding it under his arm like he wanted to impress her. Knowing Carol like I did, I figured it was working. I imagined Hettie was still smiling and holding onto her mice.

CHAPTER FOUR

One of the most scenic places in America is Atlanta in the spring when the dogwoods and azaleas are in bloom. While driving into town to pick up Hettie, I marveled at the pink and white dogwoods and the dazzling azaleas of many colors. She was excited about our day because we were going to visit the grave of her beloved husband, Joe Keller.

She would celebrate her ninety-fifth birthday in four months, and I was thinking about a special party for her. I thought about how excited she had been the year before on her birthday when I gave her the locket she had requested as a present. I remember shopping for it at several department stores and jewelers. Buying a gift for a blind person requires an innovative approach. You have to think, "How would it feel or how it would sound?" After a long search I found the perfect locket for her. It was heart shaped, and I knew she would love the implication of that design. Also, it had two little flowers etched into the silver and she could feel those. She ripped the paper off the gift like a four-year-old tearing into a Christmas present.

She pulled it out and felt it all over and said, "Wonderful, you got me a locket shaped like a heart! What are these indentations on the front?"

"Those are roses."

"Did you place your picture inside like I asked you?"

Finding a tiny picture of my face and nudging it inside the locket with tweezers was the most difficult part of the gift. "Yes, there is a picture of my handsome mug inside."

She fumbled with it until the locket was open and held it with both hands. She raised it to her mouth and kissed my picture in the open locket. Then she closed it, turned toward me and said, "Now, please put it on me and I promise I will never take it off." I struggled with hooking the clasp, but it gave me time to clear the lump in my throat caused by her sweet display of affection. She never did remove it. Two years later when she took her final breath, the locket was clutched in her hand close to her heart.

When I arrived at the nursing home, Carol greeted me with a radiant smile. She seemed happier than usual, and I asked, "What's got you so bouncy today?"

She laughed and said, "Sergeant Waters called me last night."

"Really, is that the big guy who slapped the cuffs on me?"

"It sure is."

Carol told me Hettie had tried on a few dresses that morning. "We just finished choosing one two minutes ago. Why don't you sit down and have a glass of juice while she's getting ready?"

I pulled a barstool up to the kitchen counter and said, "So is the sergeant single and available?"

Her eyes twinkled as she responded, "Yes, sireee!"

"Smells like a romance brewing to me," I said.

"It was just a telephone call, Arnie."

"How long did you talk?"

"Only fifty-one minutes."

"You mean to tell me that you timed the conversation at fifty-one minutes?"

She nodded and smiled.

"You'd better watch out. I hear the wings of cupid fluttering."

Carol laughed and then excused herself to check on Hettie. When she returned, I said, "How are we coming?"

"She's excited as a June Bug on Memorial Day. You can go on back."

My friend sat in a beige wingchair with a black book covering her lap and her fingers dancing across the pages. She had on a dress I had never seen before. When I entered the room I said, "My, my! How beautiful you are today. Please stand up and let me see that gorgeous dress." It was pale blue with white polka dots, and it had white buttons the size of quarters. Those buttons would give me trouble later that afternoon when I tried to help her.

She bounced out of the chair and spread her arms wide for a hug. I embraced her. She said, "Thank you. I love your hugs. Did you bring the blanket for our picnic?"

"Darn it! I forgot the picnic blanket."

Hettie wrinkled her brow.

"April Fool!"

She laughed and said, "Joe and I used to play that game. I've been thinking about him all morning. Thank you for taking me to visit him."

"You're welcome. This is one of those perfect spring days in Atlanta. We're going to stop and get some flowers and then we'll find a place for a picnic."

We stopped at my favorite florist. I pulled the wheelchair out of the trunk and helped Hettie into it. We entered the shop and the aroma of the flowers was breathtaking.

Hettie said, "Please stop and let me savor this moment." She took several deep breaths and the expression on her face said it all. She raised her chin slightly and her nostrils flared. Her smile seemed endless, and she crossed her arms around her chest as if she were hugging herself. She sighed, "This is wonderful. Come here and hold my hand."

I reached down and held it. The owner, Jean, approached us, "I haven't seen you in awhile, Mr. Heflin. I hope you've been feeling well."

"Just fine, Jean. It's good to see you. Say hello to my friend, Hettie Keller."

Jean reached down and shook Hettie's hand. "Welcome to Peach Blossom Florist, Mrs. Keller. What can I do for you folks today?"

As I shook Jean's hand, I said, "We're making a trip to the cemetery after we leave here and we want some fresh flowers."

Hettie said, "They're for my husband's grave."

"This is a great time of year for flowers," Jean said. "Would you like to see some roses?"

"Of course," I replied.

Jean returned and handed me a few red roses. I passed them in front of Hettie's nose so she could smell them. Hettie said, "I love roses, but let's get some different kinds of flowers, too. Can I smell them all?"

"Sure you can," I said. "What else should we get, Jean?"

"How about a few tulips?"

Hettie had decided to take control of the flower picking. She said, "Yes, bring some tulips." Jean returned and laid three orange tulips in her lap and Hettie picked one up and said, "Not any smell to these, but they feel pretty. We'll take some."

Then Jean came back with some amethyst-colored flowers. Hettie exclaimed, "What a wonderful smell! What are they?"

Jean said, "They're hyacinths, but I saved the best-smelling flower until last. Just a minute."

Hettie said, "This is so much fun. Joe will be so pleased."

I leaned down and said, "Do you know what else I brought to put on his grave, Hettie?"

"What?"

"Some quarters."

She laughed and said. "Joe's going to get a kick out of this."

Jean walked back into the room with three large pink flowers with six petals each. The petals had white borders and maroon dots on the pink portion. Hettie said, "That is the best aroma yet. What are those?"

Jean said, "They are stargazer lilies."

"That flower has an aroma that will float over the entire cemetery," Hettie said.

We returned to the car with our bundle of flowers. She said, "It seems like everything we do together is fun."

"That's because we love each other," I replied.

"You're right about that." She reached over and patted me on the leg. I had noticed Hettie loved physical contact. Whenever I held her hand, her face lit up. When I held her arm while we walked, she smiled. Whenever I gave her a hug, she said, "Thank you. It felt so good." It made me realize the touch of another human being can be a wondrous thing and should never be taken for granted.

I stopped at Kentucky Fried Chicken and picked up our lunch. We ate in a secluded park close to our destination. When I spread the blanket on the ground, Hettie said, "I want to get out of this wheelchair and sit on the grass." I helped her. She was quite a sight sitting on the navy blue blanket in her pale blue dress. She lifted her head toward the feel of the warm sun. She looked twenty years younger. There was a gentle breeze and the fresh smell of spring in the air.

I had brought a portable radio and cassette player, and I inserted one of my favorite tapes of Bette Midler. When "Wind Beneath My Wings" began to play, I said, "Hettie, this song reminds me of you." She sat straight up and turned her head toward the music. I saw a couple of tears but I knew they were the joyful kind. We ate our lunch, shared conversation and laughed a lot. Of all the times we were together, this day was one of my favorites.

I had called the caretaker of the small cemetery. He was waiting for us at his house on the property when we arrived. He found the grave and left us by ourselves. I pushed the wheelchair to the foot of Joe's grave. Hettie leaned forward and spoke to her husband: "Joe, this is my good friend, Arnold. There's no need to be jealous, because you will always be my one and only love. I am sorry I couldn't come any sooner, but there was no one to bring me. I'm sure you know how much I've missed you."

We had the flowers wrapped in dark green paper. I pulled them out and handed them to her one by one. She remembered each flower and said, "Joe, here's a hyacinth for you." Leaning forward in her wheelchair, she dropped the purple flower on his grave.

41

When the last flower, a red rose, fell from her hand I said, "Do you know what happens at moments like this?"

"What?"

"St. Peter opens the curtain in heaven and allows the person to look down at us. I believe Joe is watching us now."

"Oh, Arnold. What a beautiful thought, but right now I have to go to the bathroom."

I had been with her before in the nursing home when nature called, and I knew I had better get moving right away. I looked up and saw the caretaker on the other side of the cemetery. I yelled at him, "Can we use your bathroom?"

"Come again?" he hollered back as he cupped his hand to his ear.

I ran a few paces closer and yelled louder, "Can we use your bathroom?"

"Yeah, there's one off the front foyer."

I grabbed the handles of the wheelchair, and Hettie said, "Hurry!"

"Hold on!" I replied and began to push her through the cemetery at a trot. I had to maneuver her around and in between the graves. The ground was uneven.

She said, "This bumpy ride is making it worse."

"Hold it, Hettie! We'll be there in a minute."

We reached the car, I helped her inside, and I set the wheelchair in the trunk. I slammed it shut and jumped in the driver's seat. The house was only fifty yards away, but it looked like miles. She crossed her legs and said, "Please hurry."

I roared off and saw the caretaker look in our direction. I slammed on the brakes in front of the house, and the dust was still rising when I snatched the wheelchair out of the car. I helped Hettie into it and thanked God for the handicap ramp up the front porch. I struggled with the screen door for a few seconds and then held it open with one hand and pushed her through with the other. We entered the foyer to discover four gray doors. All shut. Jerking them open, I found the bathroom on the final attempt.

Hettie said, "Rush!"

I wheeled her inside, helped her out of the wheelchair, and guided her to the toilet.

She said, "Help me get my dress up!"

I dropped to one knee and began to fumble with the bottom white button.

"Forget the buttons, just lift up my dress."

I pulled it up to her waist.

Hettie forgot every Victorian belief she ever had and said, "Now, help me get my panties down."

Holding the dress at her waist with my left hand, I reached for the elastic on her panties with my right hand. I pulled her underwear down below her knees and lowered my eyes away from her. I said, "Hettie, I sure hope St. Peter has closed that curtain."

She laughed then screamed, "NOW JUST GET OUT OF HERE!"

I shut the door and heard her laughing.

When the bathroom door opened, a blushing Hettie entered the foyer.

I helped her back into the wheelchair. "I hope Joe Keller didn't see me with my hand on your panties."

She burst out laughing again. "I'm sure St. Peter closed that curtain. At least, I hope so."

The dust had settled by the time we returned to the car. After thanking the caretaker, we drove out of the cemetery. She said, "One time I took a ride and the car seat leaned all the way back. Does your seat lay back? I'd love to take a nap."

"Sure it does." I pulled off the road and stopped the car. "Let me fix it for you." The seat lowered all the way down, and I had brought a clean pillow anticipating she would need some rest during the day. I placed it under her head.

She said, "While I sleep could you take us to a creek?"

"What if we go to the Chattahoochee River instead?"

"Yes, wake me when we get there."

I turned the volume of Carol King's "Tapestry" tape lower and drove to the river that flows beside tall trees in a national park just north of Atlanta. There's a thirty-foot wide path that follows the winding Chattahoochee for about two miles. It is one of the great meeting places in the city. More of my friends have met their wives and husbands there than any other location in Atlanta. The park is an excellent people-watching spot: stylish singles, parents jogging behind strollers with bicycle-size tires, prancing dogs of all breeds leashed to their owners, and a montage of the young, the middle-aged, and the elderly.

When we arrived, Hettie was asleep. I parked, rolled the windows down and listened to the birds. She woke up soon and said, "Are we at the river?"

"We're here. Are you ready to take a ride along the water?"

"Yes. We must be real close to the river because I can smell it."

"The Chattahoochee is right next to the path we'll be on."

I pushed my friend in the wheelchair slowly along the river for a few hundred yards. On this lovely spring afternoon, the park was crowded with joggers, walkers and dogs all moving at their own pace, the slower people on the inside lane, and those practicing for marathons on the outside. Hettie had the navy blue blanket around her shoulders. "Find us a place where we can put our feet in the water," she said. I knew every stretch of the park and soon found the perfect spot. After spreading out the blanket, and helping Hettie out of the wheelchair, I took off our shoes at her request. We sat down with the river lapping upon the bank only two feet away.

She said, "I guess you know we're here for a reason?"

"Yes, I figured you had something in mind. You work in mysterious ways too."

She leaned forward and toward me. "I'm going to give you Maxim Number Two after I tell you a story."

"That's great, but please no more horror stories. Before you begin, let me pull part of the blanket over your shoulders. It's getting cool out here by the water."

"Could you wrap the blanket around my head too?"

I got up and settled the blanket over her hair and around her shoulders. Hettie looked like an Indian squaw. I thought, "She is one. She's one-quarter Cherokee."

"That's much better. Thank you. Now, I'm going to tell you about the worst work I've ever done in my life. It was picking the cotton. You'll never know how hard that was for our family. It's a backbreaking job because you stoop over all day long. I was young and short so I didn't have to bend down like my parents. The sun is on your back the whole time, and you have to be careful when you pull the cotton out of the boll."

"Why is that, Hettie?"

"Because the corners of the boll will cut you. Have you ever held cotton in your hand?"

"Just clothes and stuff."

"Well, believe me. Those bolls will cut you if you don't pinch the cotton just right and pull it out."

"Hettie, how could you pick cotton and not be cut?"

"I could only pick fifty pounds a day. I worked slow and deliberate because I had to feel my way around the boll to get to the cotton."

"How much could your daddy pick a day?"

"Oh, on good days he could pick four-hundred pounds, but that's working all day long."

I thought about her family working together in the dirt. "Did you go back to the house for lunch?"

"Yes, we took a lunch break around noon and then in the afternoon we walked down to the creek at the back of the property. My daddy believed you should always find a few minutes every day to spend with nature. Hardly a day went by that we didn't spend time in the woods listening to birds or dipping our feet into the creek."

"Did you ever hear any mockingbirds back in the woods?"

"You know that was my favorite bird and yes the mockingbird was with us all year long."

"What did you do at the creek?"

"We took our shoes off and put our feet in the water. I can hear and smell the Chattahoochee River. How close are we?"

"Just a couple of feet."

Hettie scooted toward the river and said, "Let's put our feet in the water."

I helped her inch forward and she lifted her dress up to her knees and stuck both feet in the river.

"Wow, that's cold!"

I sat beside her with my feet in the water too. I held her hand and she turned toward me and elevated her chin slightly, "Maxim Number Two is RELAX WITH NATURE. If you find time every day of your life to spend twenty minutes with nature, it will do wonders for you. People live at such a fast pace today. They seldom have time to rest their minds. That's what being with nature will do for you. It gives your mind a rest."

"Have you spent time with nature all your life, Hettie?"

"I sure have, and I believe it is one of the reasons for my longevity. Of course, now that I'm in the home all I can do is go sit on the back porch by myself for a little while every day."

"You do that every day?"

"Yes, even in the wintertime. Will you try relaxing with nature every day this week and see what happens? Tell me next Saturday how you feel after giving your mind a rest. Now, I'm getting cold. We'd better get back."

I dried her feet with the end of the blanket and helped her get her shoes on. I bundled the blanket around her in the wheelchair. On the way back to the car she said, "There seems to be a lot of activity out here. Tell me what you see as we leave the park."

I described the soccer field surrounded by evergreen trees, but I couldn't tell her how verdant the scene was. Explaining a Frisbee and how people tossed it about was a little difficult. We both loved dogs and I told her about the different kinds as we passed them. When I mentioned that a German shepherd was nearby, she said, "Oh! Please ask the owner to bring it to over to me."

"Okay, be back in a minute." The woman with the German shepherd was a forty-something long-legged attractive blonde with white shorts, and she was running fast. My usual form of exercise was walking, but I broke into a sprint to catch her, dodging all the people on the path. After closing the gap to a few paces, I was winded and exhausted. The pink letters DKNY about the size of a baseball were on the back of her shorts. DK was on the left side and NY was on the right. Those swinging letters kept me focused. I raced up next to her, gasping for air, and I thought, "I'll bet she's never heard this line before." Somehow, I managed to say, "Pardon me, my blind friend would like to pet your dog."

She jerked her head toward me and never broke her long stride. "Are you serious?"

With that crazy line of mine, and in my wide-eyed, open-mouthed, fatigued state, she must have thought me insane. I coughed and stuttered, "She's, She's, ninety-five years old and has, has had two German shepherds for guide, guide dogs. She would love to meet your dog."

Thank goodness she slowed to a walk and then stopped. She turned around to spot my friend. "Is that her in the wheelchair?"

Bent over double with my hands on my knees, trying to breathe, I nodded with my head until I could straighten up and talk. "Yes, that's her. Her name is Hettie and she's been blind all her life."

"Okay then, I'd be happy to take Willie to see her."

We walked toward Hettie and I said, "By the way, has anybody ever used that approach on you before?"

She had a beautiful face and a hearty laugh. "No, I've never heard that one. Is that your grandmother?"

"No, she's a friend."

The blonde runner was my height, 5' 10", and had eyes as green as the soccer field. My knees felt weak and I knew it wasn't from the running. She reached her hand out. "My name is Mary Beth."

I shook it. "My name is Arnold. It's good to meet you. Never have I chased a woman so hard."

She laughed. "Do you come here often?"

"Not as much as I used to, and this is the first time my friend has ever been here."

We approached Hettie and I said, "Mary Beth, meet my friend, Hettie Keller."

Mary Beth leaned down and reached for Hettie's hand. "Nice to meet you. I'm Mary Beth Taylor, and this is my dog, Willie."

Hettie said, "Did you name him after Willie Nelson?"

"No, I named him after an ex-boyfriend. He's gone now, but I kept the best one of the pair."

We all laughed and Hettie said, "Is he friendly? Can I pet him?"

"He's a doll baby. He loves people. Go right ahead and pet him."

From the way Hettie's hands moved over the animal's back, I knew she was a dog lover. "I had two German shepherds for guide dogs."

Mary Beth squatted down so her eyes were level with Hettie's face. "That's what Arnold said." She looked up at me and winked.

I thought, "Oh, my!"

Mary Beth talked to Hettie like she had known her all of her life. She had a lazy Southern accent that sounded like Mississippi to me.

After a few minutes of light conversation, I said, "Hettie we'd better get you back to the nursing home or they will come looking for us."

Mary Beth stood up, leaned over and gave Hettie a kiss on the cheek. "Good meeting you, Mrs. Keller."

Mary Beth turned toward me and reached her hand out to shake mine. "Maybe I'll see you out here again, Arnold. I come every Saturday at 4 o'clock."

I thought, "Could that be an invitation?" I held her hand for a few seconds and said, "I hope we meet again."

She winked and said, "I'll slow down for you next time."

Thirty minutes later, Hettie and I entered the nursing home. Carol said, "You two had a long day."

Hettie said, "We had more fun! Can't wait to tell you about it. Why, I even stuck my feet in the Chattahoochee River."

"Don't forget to tell her about the curtain, Hettie."

"What curtain was that?" Carol asked.

Hettie said, "I'll tell you later. It's the funniest story."

Carol and I helped Hettie onto her bed because she wanted to lie down before supper.

I leaned down and kissed her on the cheek and said, "Hettie, this was a day to remember. I'll see you next week."

She said, "Give your mind a rest this week. I love you."

"I love you too. Get some rest yourself, now."

On my way out Carol stopped me and said, "Sergeant Waters called me again today. We're going out next Saturday night."

I smiled and said, "Hey, it's springtime! No better season for romance."

CHAPTER FIVE

He was asleep in the corner of the box when I reached under him with both hands and lifted him out. He was smaller than a football. Immediately he began to show his affection by wiggling his behind. His tail was docked and the shaking of his rear end was like wagging his tail. Helen, the breeder, said, "Black-and-tan cocker spaniels are rare and he's the personality prize of the litter."

"Well then, I'll name him Raffles."

She looked puzzled.

"The raffle winner always gets a prize. Right?"

She nodded and said, "That's right. What a great name for a dog."

Raffles and I took our first trip together that morning. He fell asleep with his head on my thigh as we drove home.

Now, three years later, he was next to me on our trip to see Hettie. The summer months in Atlanta can be hot, and humidity can curl the quills on a porcupine. Raffles loved to stand in the passenger seat and look out the window. He propped his head on his front paws that were draped over the open window. We drove over the Chattahoochee River. I smiled as I once again thought of Mary Beth, and hoped she would be there today.

When we stopped in front of the nursing home, Raffles seemed to know this was a special occasion. His rear end was shaking with excitement. Somehow, he had a sixth sense about me showing him off to others. He was bred to be a show dog. The other four dogs in his litter were American Kennel Club champions, but Raffles had a slight overbite and did not meet AKC standards. That was fine with me because he was my show dog. Hettie was looking forward to meeting him for the first time. I put Raffles on a leash and we entered the front door to be welcomed by Carol.

When I placed our lunch on the counter, Raffles went straight to her and began to wiggle his behind next to her legs. Carol said, "What a handsome dog," and she squatted down to pet him. "Look at him shake that bootie. Why I have never seen a dog move his behind so fast. What's his name?"

"Raffles, and he's the best dog I've ever had."

She stood. "Before you go back to see Hettie, I have to tell you where Chucky took me last night."

"You call that big man, Chucky? That's funny. Three months ago it was Sergeant Waters. Two months ago it was Charles and last month it was Chuck. Today it's Chucky. Where did you go?"

"We went to Chastain Park to hear Ella Fitzgerald."

"Oh, I think she's the greatest. I heard her sing at the New Orleans Jazz Fest a few years ago. Did you enjoy yourselves?"

"Best time I've ever had and Ella's voice is still singing in my ears."

"Chastain is so romantic, Carol. You walk down the grassy hillside, and see all those candles sparkling on the tables covered with white cloth. I can imagine how clear Ella's voice was to you both last night. Are you in love?"

A tear dribbled out of her right eye, ran down her cheek and fell on the white collar of her uniform. Her lips quivered but her eyes sparkled. She couldn't say a word. She nodded. I dropped the leash and stepped forward and put my arms around her. "I'm so happy for you."

She sighed, "He's wonderful."

I kissed her on the cheek, grabbed the lunch, picked up the leash and told Raffles, "Break!" He jumped up from a sitting position and pranced down the corridor to Hettie's room, keeping pace with my left foot. Hettie was reading as usual. I said, "Raffles, say hello to my friend, Hettie Keller."

She said, "Hey Raffles!" He was trained not to jump up on people so he went straight for her legs and snuggled up next to them shaking his behind. She smiled, reached down and petted him. "He's so happy to see me!" Raffles licked her leg just above the ankle. She said, "He licked me."

"Raffles, sit! Go ahead and pet him, Hettie, while he's sitting down."

She ran her fingers through his coat. I could tell she was delighted to have her hands on a dog again. After I gave Hettie a hug, we both played with Raffles and then all of us ate our lunch. After we finished, Raffles went to sleep lying next to her chair.

Hettie said, "What would we have done without the dogs in our lives?"

"I can't imagine. Please tell me about your first dog."

She smiled, leaned back in her chair and raised her chin. "The first dog I remember was a German shepherd named Sarge. My daddy said Sarge was my shadow."

I thought, "She's never seen a shadow."

She took a sip of her iced tea and dabbed the corners of her mouth with a napkin. "I was around six and Momma asked me to walk down to the watermelon patch and pick out a small one for supper. Sarge went with me. From our back porch there was a slight hill all the way down to the bottomland. I was excited and hungry so I ran back up the hill with the watermelon cradled in my arms. I tripped and fell right on top of the melon and smashed it. I sat there crying and Sarge started licking my face. I didn't know if he was licking me because I was crying or because he liked watermelon."

I laughed. "That's a neat story."

Hettie smiled, "Now it's your turn to tell me about your first dog."

"Well, I was six-years-old too, and my dog was part sheep dog. He had long hair drooping down over his eyes."

"I know the kind you're talking about. I've felt one before," Hettie said.

"His name was Skipper, and he loved to chase cars. My mom had just come home from the hospital with my newborn baby sister, and they both were lying in bed. My brother and I were playing in the front yard when Skipper went after a car. This time he came too close and was run over right in front of us. I raced inside the house and yelled, 'Skipper's dead! Skipper's dead!'"

"Mom said, 'I can't get up now. Call your dad at the office.'"

"He answered the phone and heard me crying, 'What's wrong Son? What's wrong?'"

"I sobbed incoherently, 'Skipper's dead. Skipper's dead.'"

"My dad thought I said, 'Sister's dead. Sister's dead.'"

Hettie gasped, "Oh no."

"Dad shouted, 'What happened?'"

"I continued to cry, 'Skipper was run over in the street.'"

"Dad yelled, 'What the hell was your sister doing in the street?'"

"I said, 'Not Sister! Skipper!'"

Hettie shook her head, "My word. What terrible confusion that was."

"I know. Dad left work early, came home and helped us bury Skipper in the back yard."

The smell of fresh hot coffee drifted into the room before Carol did. She walked in holding two steaming mugs. "Thought you two story-tellers might like this."

"Thanks Carol. It's just what we wanted," Hettie said.

Watching Carol walk back down the corridor, I could tell she was in love. There's something about love that changes people. Their eyes are brighter, their smiles are wider, their steps are springier, and nothing can rattle their serenity. Hiding the look of love is like trying to sweep an elephant under a rug. I missed the feeling. There's nothing better than being in love. Nothing at all.

I was ready for more stories, "Tell me about your guide dogs, Hettie."

"I picked up my first guide dog in the summer of 1944, and it changed my life forever."

"Why?"

"A guide dog gives you freedom and independence. Your dog opens up a whole new world for you. You're able to walk about the city at a normal pace with confidence. From the moment I left Detroit with my dog, Sarge …"

"Excuse me, your first guide dog was named Sarge just like the dog you had as a child? Did you name your guide dog?"

"No, he was already named when Leader Dogs gave him to me."

"Was Leader Dogs the place that trained the guide dog?"

"That's right," Hettie said. "I went through a four week training program by myself there in Detroit, Michigan, before I could bring Sarge home."

I said, "What a coincidence your guide dog had the same name as your first dog."

"Arnold, it was much more than a coincidence. The older you get, the more you realize that God arranges for inevitable circumstances and he places certain people along the path of your life's journey. He puts them there for one reason and that is to help you. Do you think we met just by chance?"

I paused and thought about the hundreds of people that the Center for the Visually Impaired could have sent me to visit. "No, there must be a reason we came together."

Hettie said, "You're right and sometimes you may not know what the reason is until years later. However, I know why you came to me."

"Why?"

"To bring me joy before I die."

I felt my throat getting tight. "Thank you, Hettie. That's quite a compliment."

"I remember the first time you called me. I was lying in bed and had just finished my prayers. I asked God, 'This home is hard for me. Please make my life easier.' Then the phone rang and I heard that deep southern voice of yours. By the way, what do you think about the last maxim, RELAX WITH NATURE?"

"Hettie, that's a fantastic maxim. I love it!"

"Why?"

"Commercial real estate is high stress. The twenty minutes I spend every day relaxing with nature reduces my level of anxiety. Just like you said, it gives your mind a rest."

"Good! How about your prayers? Are they working?"

"Yes, but I'm learning to accept God's time table when it comes to prayer."

Hettie laughed, "They're working then because you've learned a most valuable lesson. God answers prayers on His schedule, not ours. This sounds like a good time for me to give you Maxim Number Three." She raised her chin slightly and said, "LESS IS MORE."

"Does that mean I have to sell my big, new SUV and get me a used Volkswagen Bug?" Do you know what a bug looks like? She made a semicircle with her hand and I said, "You know the car."

Hettie smiled and leaned back in her chair. "What I mean by LESS IS MORE is this: The fewer distractions you have in your life, the more opportunity you have to develop your own sense of purpose. God gave us the gift of life for a reason. We each have our own destiny to fulfill. God will lead you toward that destiny and He will bring people into your life that will help you find it, but He won't accomplish it for you. You have to do it yourself."

"Did you accomplish your destiny, Hettie?"

"Oh yes, many times over. I taught hundreds of people how to read Braille. My destiny has been achieved. Do you know yours, Arnold?"

"I'm not sure."

"That's okay," Hettie said. "You'll find your destiny. And when you do, your discovery will be absolute. It will be unmistakable. There will be no doubts. Now, let's get back to talking about our dogs."

"All right, tell me more about your first guide dog. What kind of dog was it?"

"Sarge was a male German shepherd-collie cross."

"That had to be a great dog. Those are two wonderful breeds. When I broke into your conversation you were saying, 'from the moment I left Detroit with my dog Sarge …'"

"Yes, from then on I had the ability to move around Atlanta and feel safe in spite of the street cars and automobile traffic. Also, the pace of my walking increased as opposed to my walking behind a tapping cane." Hettie reached for her white cane beside her chair and held it toward me. "Please take this in your hand."

I accepted the cane. She said, "Stand up. Close your eyes and walk to the bathroom door and then come back to your chair using only the cane."

Following her instructions, and inching the cane along in front of me, I found my way back to the chair. "That took quite a while."

"Now you understand," Hettie said. "Before my dog the only sight I had was through the cane. I could slowly walk down the street and use it to tell where I was in relationship to buildings, objects and curbs. I can't tell you how many times I walked into something or stumbled off of curbs. While you're holding it in your hand, your sense and feel of your surroundings is only as long as the length of your cane. I was forty-four- years old when I got on a train in Atlanta and rode up to Detroit to be trained with Sarge."

"Did you get your dog the first day you got there?"

"Oh, no. The first thing they do is train you on how to use a dog."

I was fascinated. "You mean like what commands to give the dog?"

"Yes, commands are part of the training, but even more important is how you relate to your dog. They teach you to have total trust and confidence in the animal. They even teach the dog what is known as intelligent disobedience. That means if you give your guide dog a command that would place you in harm's way, the dog will not obey the order."

"That's cool. So if you told your dog to hurry up and by hurrying up you would be in danger, the dog would disobey?"

"Exactly! If I said,'Hup up,' which means hurry on, and the faster pace would put me in jeopardy, the dog would not accept the order."

"Did you ever give your dog an order, and the dog disobeyed?"

Hettie got up out of her chair. "Yes, I have a story about intelligent disobedience, but first let me stretch." She did this whenever we sat down for a long period of time. She stood erect with her feet about eighteen inches apart and reached up to the ceiling with both hands like a referee signaling a touchdown. She held her arms upright for a minute or so and every few seconds she stood up on her tiptoes. She lowered her arms to her shoulders and stretched them out with her palms facing the floor. Then she rotated her torso to the left of center, back to center, and then to the right. Then she stood with her feet together, bent forward from the waist and reached toward the floor with both hands. I counted her repetitions this time and she did twelve of those. Her total routine took no more than three or four minutes. She sat back in the chair and announced with a grin, "Okay, I'm good to go now."

"Hettie, no wonder you're so limber and move around with ease. I'm impressed with your exercise routine. Now, tell me about the time when your dog didn't obey you."

"It happened a week after I got back from Detroit with Sarge. We were crossing Boulevard Street near the hospital. Do you know where that is?"

"Sure, there's a lot of traffic on that road."

"Sarge and I were caught in the middle of the street with traffic going by us on both sides. We waited for the longest time and I became impatient. The dog doesn't make the decision when to cross the road. That's up to the owner. I listened for the sound of cars and I didn't hear any engine noise so I thought the road was safe. I gave Sarge the command to go. He didn't budge. I stepped ahead without him and was hit by a car."

"Oh no! How bad were you hurt?"

"I broke both legs, several ribs, and my right arm. I was in the hospital for six weeks. Do you know what I did when I was physically able to work my dog again?"

"What?"

"I got Sarge and we walked to that same intersection. We crossed the street three times together."

"You're very courageous."

"There's a fine line between courage and stupidity, but in this case I had to prove to Sarge and myself that we could do it together."

"Hettie, I know how close Raffles and I are, but your connection with your dogs was on another level."

"The best way I can explain the relationship is that you become one with your dog. Sarge became my eyes, my constant companion and great friend. My guide dogs were my salvation. Together for forty-eight years, we moved all around Atlanta, which is a busy place as you know."

"How many guide dogs have you had?"

She was silent for a few seconds and then she said, "I've had five dogs from 1944 to 1992. The first was Sarge, the German shepherd-collie cross. Then sometime in the mid-50s Sarge died. I went back to Leader Dogs and trained with a male collie named, Lassie. I kept Lassie for ten years or so until he got sick. Joe and I had to put him to sleep. Then I returned to Leader Dogs and got Judy, a female German shepherd cross. Judy was my most cherished dog. She was my first female dog, and we had a special bond. She was with me when Joe died, and she helped ease the pain of my loneliness.

"Judy always slept on the floor on my side of the bed. The night of Joe's funeral when I said, 'Bedtime' she led me into the bedroom. I put on my pajamas and got into bed, and Judy was on the floor. I started thinking about Joe and how he never let me go to sleep without giving me a kiss and saying, 'Good night. I love you.' I started crying out loud and I heard Judy get up off the floor. The next thing I knew she was beside me in bed licking the tears off of my cheeks. It reminded me of Sarge licking my face when I was a kid. From that night on we always slept together.

Just before I went to sleep she nudged over and licked my cheek. Judy's love took over where Joe's left off."

I had tears rolling down my face and it was hard for me not to cry out loud. There was no way I could say a word.

"Judy and I became even closer after Joe passed. When she died two years later it liked to have killed me. I was seventy-eight-years old, and I decided I couldn't go through the pain of losing another dog. I told the Center for the Visually Impaired, 'No more dogs for me,' but they talked me out of it. I went back to Leader Dogs in 1977 and got a female Labrador retriever named Chami. Judy was a hard act to follow, but Chami was a wonderful dog too. She was a mind reader. She knew which way I was going before I spoke a command. Then suddenly, at the early age of five, she died."

I was sitting there wiping the tears off my face. I had to blow my nose, but I knew if I did I would completely lose it. The lump in my throat was huge. It was too much of a struggle. My emotions won and I began to sob. Raffles came over and rubbed up against me and I cried even more. Hettie cried too. We both sobbed uncontrollably. We reached for each other's hands and held them while we wept. We took deep breaths. I reached for more tissues and wiped her tears away and then mine. After a few minutes, Carol came into the room and knelt down beside us with her arms around our shoulders. We wailed even louder. Only a dog lover would understand. There are dog owners and there are dog lovers. Hettie and I were dog lovers.

It took us a few minutes to compose ourselves while Carol slipped out of the room. "I haven't cried like that since Joe passed." Hettie said.

"Same here. I haven't shed that many tears since my mom died in 1981."

"There's nothing in the world wrong with crying. It's good for you."

"There was a time in my life when I never cried out loud, but that's changed. Let me ask you, was Chami your last dog then?"

"Oh no. I got one more guide dog after she died. I went back to Leader Dogs in 1981 and they trained me with another German shepherd cross, a female named Josie."

"Is Leader Dogs still in Detroit?"

"No they moved nearby to the smaller town of Rochester, Michigan many years ago."

"Did you have to pay for the dogs or the training?"

"Not a dime. Not even for the travel or the board while you're there. They are funded by the Lions Club and through private donations. Please add them to your contribution list."

"I will and I'll ask my friends to do the same."

"Thank you."

"You're welcome. How long was Josie your companion?"

"She was with me until 1992, the year I came here to the home."

"So, you had guide dogs for almost fifty years?"

"That's right," Hettie said. "They were my eyes and friends and I'm sure they contributed to my long life. You're so good with math: Let's say I patted my dogs four times an hour for the sixteen hours I was awake. How many times would I have petted them in my life?"

"Okay, you patted them sixty-four times a day for three-hundred sixty-five days, which would be around twenty-three thousand times a year. And you had guide dogs for forty-eight years." I paused a few seconds, "About a million times."

"A million times! Come here Raffles," she said. Raffles went over and snuggled up to Hettie's leg.

She lowered her head down toward Raffles and gave him a pat on his back. "Now, that's one million, and one. That one is meant for your good luck, Raffles, and for the good fortune of your dear owner."

"Hettie, don't get me crying again. I don't think I can stand any more."

We both laughed. Raffles gave her a lick on the leg and I gave her a kiss on the cheek. I took her shoes off and helped get into her bed. I pulled the afghan over her legs and said, "See you next week. I love you, Hettie."

"I love you too, Arnold."

When I left, Carol was busy in another room. I grabbed the notepad by the phone sitting under the yellow cabinets in the kitchen, and wrote her a short message: "Carol, sorry I missed you going out the door. I have a dinner suggestion for you and your beau. Take the Sergeant to Chucky Cheese. See you next Saturday, Arnie."

Raffles had too much excitement for one day and he fell asleep on the passenger seat, but I woke him up when we got to the river, "Want to go for a walk?" His sleepy eyes opened and he wiggled with excitement. I glanced at my watch and it was 3:50 p.m. Raffles and I hit the wide trail on the Chattahoochee River a few minutes later.

We walked here often, but today my thoughts were on Mary Beth. When we first met three months ago, I was infatuated. Her charming personality and warm smile won me over. I was anxious to see her. When she told me she came to the river every Saturday at 4 p.m., I felt certain that was an invitation to meet her again. She even made the point that she had broken up with her boyfriend. With Raffles by my side for the next hour I looked for her, just like I had every Saturday for the past three months. I had spent no more than thirty minutes with her on the afternoon we met, but I could not get her out of my mind. One night this week, I dreamed about her. We were playing soccer together on the field by the Chattahoochee River. She made the winning goal with a minute remaining in the game. We gave each other a high five. She said, "A winning goal deserves more than that – why don't you give me a hug?" I walked over and put my arms around her. I did not want to let her go. When I awoke I was still hugging her in my dreams. I missed her. No green eyes. No long legs. No warm smile. No Mary Beth.

Raffles and I returned to the car and I played Bill Withers' great recording of "Ain't No Sunshine." I reached over to pet Raffles. I thought, "One million and two, and I remembered Hettie's wish for my good fortune. If she got her wish, I'd see Mary Beth again.

CHAPTER SIX

When I walked into Hettie's room on a rainy afternoon she bounced out of her chair and said, "Let me give you a hug. I've missed you."

"Okay, but let me put away my raincoat because it's pouring down out there."

She said, "I've been listening to raindrops dancing on the windows all morning."

After hanging the coat in her closet, I gave her a warm embrace and said, "What do you say we start this afternoon off with a steaming cup of hot chocolate?"

"You always have the best ideas. You're so much fun."

"Thank you, so are you. Excuse me while I get us a mug. Marshmallows as usual?"

Hettie smiled, "You know I love them. Please get me a handful this time."

The sweet aroma enticed Hettie to take a deep breath and smile as we both sat back in our chairs. I took my first sip of the warm chocolate and crossed my legs. Hettie's sweater was falling off of her left shoulder so I stood and said, "Let me get your sweater straight."

She smiled, "You look after me. Don't you?"

"Absolutely!"

I returned to my chair. Hettie looked peaceful and happy. It appeared to be the perfect time to talk about her one and only love, Joe Keller. "Hettie, tell me how you fell in love with Joe?" I sat back and listened as she told her love story. Hettie always smiled when Joe's name was mentioned. She had a broad grin as she began to tell about their love.

"What better way for two blind people to meet than to bump into each other? That's the way I met my future husband. I was getting off a streetcar in Atlanta while he was boarding. It was just as clumsy as it sounds. I tripped and fell off the bottom step while he was standing at the curb waiting to get on. Only the people crowded behind Joe kept us both from falling on the sidewalk together. It was such an embarrassing moment for me, but when you're blind you get use to awkward situations. We were entangled and I said, 'Please forgive me. I cannot see.'

"Joe laughed and said, 'That's obvious.'

"Right away I thought, 'Wise guy!'

" 'I'm kidding you,' he said. 'I'm blind too. Chances are I was standing too close to the streetcar when you got off. Are you okay?'

"His voice sounded warm and friendly. 'Yes, I'm fine.'

" 'My name is Joe Keller. What's yours?'

" 'Hettie Higginbotham.'

" 'Please let me buy you a cup a coffee.' Joe said. 'There's a park down the hill that has some benches.'

"We took our first step together that afternoon, and we walked side by side for the next thirty-eight years. Joe was legally blind, but he saw large objects. The best way to describe his sight is that he would not walk into a tree like I did occasionally, but he might trip over smaller things like the brooms he sold for a living. We met in the fall of 1937. Mother and I lived together in Cabbagetown. My father died in 1932, and my brother, Charlie, was in prison for public drunkenness. We struggled like everyone else did during the 30s except for the rich.

"Joe and I sat in the park and talked for hours. There was a café nearby, and Joe walked over there and he brought back an egg salad sandwich that we shared. I've thought about the first day with Joe many times. It's funny, but I can't recall a lot of what we talked about. I remember him helping me put my sweater on and how warm his arm was when it brushed up against my shoulder. The sensation I felt then is something that I'll never forget. He walked me home and helped me at the curbs. The warmth of his hands seemed to go right through me.

"I'd never brought a man home with me before, and mother was surprised and ornery. After she went to bed, Joe and I sat on the front porch swing and rocked. We talked for hours. Our hands seemed to fall together, and Joe's forefinger traced a pattern over the top of my hand. His touch was so gentle.

" 'I wish I could ask you to spend the night on the sofa,' I whispered.

"Joe replied, 'Don't believe I'd want to confront your mother in the morning. Thanks, but no thanks.' "

"After he left I went to bed and thought about him. No sleeping for me. I grabbed my blanket and went outside where the owls were in concert. I curled up in the swing and the scent of Joe and jasmine still hung in the cool air. I had never had anything like a boyfriend. Oh, I'd had men grope at me before. Somehow they felt because of my vision impairment, they could get away with it. Not so. I always raised my cane and yelled, 'Don't you dare touch me!' Once, on a streetcar the conductor stopped as soon as I screamed. He came back and threw the man off. That's what the passengers told me.

"After we met, Joe came over to the house every night about the time mother went to bed. We swung on the porch and talked about everything in the world. Six months later Joe proposed to me one spring evening while we were swinging. He said, 'Hettie, let's get married this summer.'

"I said, 'Okay, but you know we'll be old before we know it.'

" 'Why?'

"Joe was a man of few words, and I replied, 'Because time flies when we're together.' He gave me a big hug. I said, 'Kiss.' I puckered my lips and he gave me a big one. Wouldn't you know it, mother came out the door that very second.

"The next day, Joe tied a little bell to the door handle. I thought it was such a great idea that I asked him to get me a bell too. From then on we both carried a short-handle bell in our pockets. Whenever we wanted a kiss, we rang the bell. Not only did we have lots of fun ringing our "kissing bells," we resolved a few disagreements by shaking them. The people living next to us must have thought it was Christmas every day because there was a whole lot of jingling going on. I bet there would be far fewer divorces if couples used "kissing bells" like we did. There were three wondrous discoveries of my early adult life: "kissing bells," guide dogs and a big old softhearted guy named Joe Keller.

"My mother worked as a maid for a judge who agreed to marry us. Mother and I walked into town and shopped for a wedding dress at Rich's Department Store. On the big day, I walked into the judge's office with Mother and Joe. The judge said, 'Hettie, you are so beautiful.' I got goose bumps all over me. After the short ceremony he said those words that I can still hear late at night when I can't sleep, 'I now pronounce you man and wife.' The judge gave us a generous wedding present. He got us a room for two nights at the Winecoff Hotel on Peachtree Street, and he gave us twenty dollars.

"Joe and I were like two kids although we were both in our late 30s. We were so nervous after the wedding that we didn't go to the hotel but spent all afternoon walking around the city. We returned to the same park bench where we had shared the sandwich on the first day we met. Mother had packed a small suitcase for me and I asked her to put my clarinet in there. We sat on the park bench and I played while Joe sang. People walking by saw me in my white wedding dress and they came over and joined us in the singing. Joe was from Brooklyn and I played "Dixie" for him. He didn't know the words, but the people from Atlanta sure did. Everyone sang loud that afternoon. In honor of my husband, I played "Battle Hymn of the Republic." "When the sun went down I played the last song, "You Belong to Me."

"We walked back up the hill to the Winecoff. I will never forget when we entered the hotel a man said, 'Why, you must be Mr. and Mrs. Joe Keller.' It was the first time anyone ever called me Mrs. Keller. Then I realized that Helen Keller and I had the same last name. She went to Perkins Institute too.

"After we ate dinner, they led us up to our room, number 315 located in front of the elevator. Joe and I felt around the room with our canes and hands. We had two chairs, a table, a dresser, and the biggest bed I ever slept on. There was a radio on a table next to the bed and Joe turned it on and the music just floated around us. The tub in the bathroom seemed big enough for a small family. I had never owned a nightgown until mother bought me one at Rich's. She told me to put it on before Joe and I went to bed.

"I said, 'Joe, I'm going to take a bath now.' My heart was racing when I brought my small suitcase into the bathroom and filled up the tub. The warm water felt so good. I lay back and thought, 'Dear God, thank you for bringing me Joe Keller.'

"Soon I heard Joe ringing his bell, and I said, 'Coming Mr. Keller.' Joe and I had never lain down next to each other, and only my love for him kept me on steady feet. I dried off with a towel as large as a rug and pulled the slippery nightgown over my head. I had to do something to relieve my tension and calm my nerves so I reached back into the suitcase. When I opened the door I held the clarinet to my lips and played "Jingle Bells." Joe Keller couldn't stop laughing even after I rang my bell several times.

"We slept way into the afternoon. When we got up we opened the windows and heard the streetcars. We knew our room was on the Peachtree Street side of the hotel. We pulled our table and chairs underneath the window. We drank coffee and listened to the noises of a city in a hurry. Joe and I both loved to listen to "people sounds." Saturdays were bustling in Atlanta because everyone came into town for shopping. Davidson's Department Store was next door to the hotel, and the streetcar stopped right below our window. We talked and laughed all afternoon listening to the chatter of the crowd below. I put my wedding dress on and took my clarinet to the open window and began to play. Before long people were shouting up to us, 'Congratulations! Best Wishes!'

"I've often wondered if the people in the adjacent rooms ever complained about bells ringing. What a grand memory!

"Since our marriage was childless we were able to devote all of our time to each other. Without sight, you tend to withdraw from people anyway, but Joe and I found strength together. We had a great marriage. Sometimes, just before I go to sleep, I hear the sound of those kissing bells. It always brings a smile and a warm feeling of happiness. Arnold, I loved Joe more than I can explain in words."

"Hettie, what a delightful tale. I've always wanted to write a book. The life of you and Joe Keller would make a good story."

"Why don't you write one?"

"I'm so involved in commercial real estate. I don't have time to write a postcard."

"When did you discover your love for writing?"

"When I was eight or nine."

"We had a roll-top desk where mom kept her stationery and envelopes. I was fascinated with the magic of how the rolling top disappeared.

"Mom said, 'the desk is not a toy. If you want to write, then it's okay to open it.'

"I stacked pillows on a chair so I was high enough to write. I watched the top disappear and picked up her black quill pen. At first I wrote about simple things, like playing marbles. Later I experimented with words that rhymed. On Mother's Day when I was nine, I wrote a poem to go with a box of candy my brother and I had bought for her. It went like this:

> 'We got you something sweet
> to lay at your pretty feet
> on this Sunday in May
> We love you every day.'

"How we got the candy is a neat story. About three years earlier my father decided he did not want to work inside a factory anymore. He wanted to be an outside salesman. It took him awhile to get going and earn some money, and until he did we had some tough financial times. The Monday before Mother's Day, my brother, Alan, and I walked to school with a quarter in each of our pockets for lunch. I said, 'Alan, why don't we skip lunch every day this week and save the quarters and then get mom a big box of candy for Mother's Day?'

"He was a year younger than I, Alan said, 'Okay, but what will we do while everyone goes to lunch?'

"We'll sneak out on the playground and play.'

"Neither of us realized how hungry two little boys could be from going without a meal. I remember both of us sitting on a curb next to the playground. Alan said, 'Gosh, I'm really hungry.'

"Me too! Do you have like a knot in your stomach?'

"Yeah, and it hurts. Can we eat some grass?'

"No, it might make us sick. Besides, it's Thursday and we only have one more day.' I put my arm around his shoulder and said, 'We can do it.'

"On Saturday morning Alan and I ate a big breakfast and then we walked to the drugstore and shopped for candy. We had two dollars and fifty cents and it was enough to get a large yellow box of Whitman's Chocolates, along with wrapping paper and tape. We wrapped the candy and hid it under our bed. After we got back from church on Sunday, I grabbed my three-year-old sister's hand and took her back into our bedroom and we got the sack with the poem and the gift. I told Sissy, 'Now let's walk into the living room, give Mom the surprise, and together we'll all say 'Happy Mother's Day!'

"Mom and Dad were sitting on the sofa. We sat on the floor and watched while Mom reached into the sack and pulled out the poem. When she read it a few tears ran down her cheeks and Dad gave her a handkerchief. I felt bad that my poem had made her cry and I thought, 'The next time I'll write something funny.'

"Alan said, 'Open the candy.'

"I gave him a stare and a poke as Mom unwrapped her present.

"When she saw this big box of chocolates she looked at Dad and nodded with approval. She thought he had bought the candy. Dad had a puzzled look on his face and shook his head no. Back then, two dollars and fifty cents wasn't just lying around our house. Mom looked at me.

"Where did you get the money?'

"I glanced at Alan, but he dropped his eyes to the floor. 'We saved our lunch money every day last week.'

"Mom asked, 'How did you eat?'

"Alan finally decided to help. 'We didn't eat lunch all week. I was so hungry that I wanted to eat grass, but Arnold wouldn't let me.'

"Now Mom really began to cry. We all jumped up off the floor and tried to hug her at the same time. Dad moved over close to her with the handkerchief again. For the rest of that day every time Mom looked at Alan or me she would cry again.

"Lying in bed that night, I thought about how my poem had brought tears to her eyes. Years later I wrote for the high school paper and graduated from Auburn University with a degree in Journalism and English. Two newspapers made me an offer, but unfortunately the pay was so low I couldn't accept either job. Instead, I got into sales like my father and I have had a great time selling commercial real estate."

"Do you think you will ever write a book, Arnold?"

"I don't know. I've been too busy to think about it."

"How old was your dad when he changed careers?"

"Somewhere around thirty-five. Why?"

"This is the perfect time to give you the fourth maxim." She leaned forward in her chair, lifted her chin slightly and said, "It is PASSION BRINGS PURPOSE."

"Your dad found his passion when he changed jobs. You've known of your passion since you were nine-years-old. Remember, it's never too late to discover your passion. Doubt will always find a way into your mind. It's natural. The way you overcome uncertainty and doubt is through passion. When you have passion you can walk right through the wall of doubt. Passion is the spark that ignites the drive, energy and purpose in our life. How many successful people have you met who were not passionate about their careers?"

"You know Hettie, I don't believe I've met a single one."

"That wouldn't surprise me. Passion brings a certain purpose to our lives. There is no limit to what you can accomplish with passion. If you are living a life without passion it's like trying to drive a car without a steering wheel. Although you've done a good job of suppressing your passion for writing."

"Hettie, how can you tell that writing is my passion?"

"It's easy. I listen to every word you say. The sound of your voice, your inflections, your delivery, they all tell me something about you. I've heard your enthusiasm about real estate, high-rise office buildings, and being involved in the development of Atlanta. I've also listened to you tell me about propping pillows up on a chair and writing. There is no question in my mind which of those two you love the most. I know that writing is your true passion."

"I know I can make a living leasing and selling office buildings, but I don't know about writing."

"Your passion will carry through those doubts. Trust me."

I was dumbfounded. My love for words and dreams of writing stories someday were my deepest thoughts. I had shared them with no one. How in the world could Hettie know?

A beaming Carol came into the room and set two mugs of coffee on the table. She had a hand towel draped over one arm.

"Okay, my favorite storytellers, I brought a towel just in case you were talking about your dogs again."

Everyone laughed. She sat on Hettie's bed and wiped her brow. I spotted something glittering.

"Carol do you have something new on your left hand?"

The sparkle in her eyes telegraphed her answer. "Chucky gave me this ring last night."

Hettie said, "Please let me feel it."

Carol stretched her arm out over Hettie's lap. Hettie's fingers encircled the ring, "Why, this ring is huge."

I said, "Let me see it too. Wow, that's a beautiful diamond."

Looking at Carol, I saw tears beginning to well. I pointed to the hand towel. She smiled and dabbed her eyes.

Hettie asked, "Have you set a wedding date?"

"Not yet, but we want you both to come."

"My, my, I haven't been to a wedding since Joe and I got married in the summer of '38. Goodness gracious, that's over fifty years ago. I'll need something to wear. And what can I do with my hair?"

I said my good-byes and left Hettie and Carol talking about wedding plans. I glanced at my watch. It was 3:30.

As usual, I got to the Chattahoochee River at 4 o'clock and started walking down the path. Every Saturday since Mary Beth and I had met, I left the home and timed my visit to the river so I would arrive at the time she said she usually got there. I have always been surprised by how many encounters are just pure chance and good old-fashioned luck. You're standing in line at the grocery counter, someone behind you drops a loaf of bread and you pick it up and start a conversation. You fall off a streetcar and into the arms of your future husband.

I smiled when I pictured Hettie standing in the doorway of the bathroom playing "Jingle Bells" on the clarinet. I thought about how perceptive my dear friend was to know about my love of writing by listening to the sound of my voice. When I first saw her in the den with the Braille book in her lap, I had sensed something special about her, but I never imagined she would have had such a profound influence on my life.

From behind me I heard, "Pardon me mister, but there's a friend of mine who would like for you to pet her alligator."

I recognized Mary Beth's voice right away and smelled the soft scent of her perfume as I turned to see her. She looked even better than I had remembered. She was dressed in white: shorts, shirt, socks, shoes and headband. Eyes still green and legs still long. I laughed. "That's the craziest line I've ever heard."

Mary Beth said, "No, I've heard one crazier than that before. It had something to do with a blind friend petting a dog. How have you been, Arnold?"

"Life's been good and it's getting better. How are you doing? Where's your dog, Willie?"

"I'm good now, but I've had a tough four months. Thank you for asking about Willie – he is being groomed."

People were dodging around us on the path, and Mary Beth said, "Follow me." She led me to a bench a few feet away. Her eyes sparkled as she looked at me. "Is Hettie with you today?"

"No, I left her at the home a few minutes ago."

"How's she doing?"

"She's fine, but please tell me what's been giving you a hard time?"

"I've been with my grandmother in Taos, New Mexico. She's been sick for a long time and she died last Monday."

"Oh, I'm so sorry. Do you feel like talking about her?"

"Her name was Nettie. When you introduced me to Hettie, I thought about Grandma, and how similar their names were. She was a landscape artist of Western scenes and her husband died during World War II. She was eighty-five-years-old, and we had always been close."

I listened as Mary Beth told me about Nettie. We walked to our cars. It felt like I had found a lost friend, and she seemed happy to be with me. We made a dinner date for the next Saturday. My heart was racing as we held hands for a few minutes while we walked to the car and said our goodbyes. I could not believe the feeling in my stomach – it felt as though I had not had anything to eat for days.

The day was brighter and the sky bluer as I left the parking lot. I turned the radio on and Willie Nelson was singing "Good-Hearted Woman." Talk about luck. What were the odds of meeting a woman who was jogging with her German shepherd that your blind friend wanted to pet?

CHAPTER SEVEN

At 8:30 on Monday morning my secretary said, "Mr. Heflin, there's a woman named Mary Beth Taylor on line two for you."

I thought, "I hope she's not calling to cancel our date on Saturday night." I picked up the phone and said, "Good morning, did you ever find anyone to pet the alligator of your friend?"

Her hearty laughter eased my tension. "Your voice sounds even deeper over the telephone. Are you busy now?"

Holding the phone at arm's length I said, "Jinny, cancel that order on the two million hogs. Hold all of my calls until I'm finished with this alligator dealer." Mary Beth had a deep voice herself and a sexy, throaty laugh.

She said, "You're funny. I've seen you twice. Both times you had a smile on your face and a glint in your eye. It's too bad that Mrs. Keller can't see those brown eyes sparkle."

"Hettie's intuition is multiplied tenfold. The depth of her understanding is beyond description. Mary Beth, you'd be shocked at how well she knows me by just listening to me talk."

Mary Beth said, "With all of her other senses magnified, she must listen in a way that we could never understand. I can't wait to hear more about her. My father called me last night and he's coming through town from Mississippi on Saturday afternoon. I want to see you this weekend. Will Friday night work for you?"

"Absolutely."

"I'm going to leave the arrangements up to you. Just tell me where we're going so I'll know what to wear."

Having already thought about our first date, my reply was immediate. "We'll have dinner at the Ritz Carlton downtown. Afterwards we'll walk a block up Peachtree Street to the Plaza Hotel and ride the exterior glass elevator up to the seventieth floor. From the lounge on the top floor, we'll have a great view of Atlanta, and on the way home we'll stop by the Hideaway and dance."

Mary Beth replied, "Sounds perfect. Why don't you pick me up around seven?"

She gave me directions to her house and I said, "See you Friday evening. Have a good week, Mary Beth."

"You too, Arnold."

It was one of the worst weeks of my life. Dad called me at the office on Tuesday evening and told me he had been diagnosed with Merkel cell cancer. Right after our conversation I called my friend, Dr. Wilson Brown, Sr. and asked him about my father. He told me Merkel cell was a virulent form of skin cancer. He said it was rare and fatal.

Although my father was eighty-four, I had never thought about losing him. After all, his dad had lived to be ninety-nine. He was such an important part of my life, and always a great inspiration to my siblings and me. Somebody told me one day that you never become a man until your father dies. I thought, "Then I'm totally happy being a boy."

After the call I left the office and drove to a secluded spot to relax with nature. I had tried meditation before Hettie gave me the maxim, but was never able to master the technique. For some reason being with nature and away from the sounds of the city brought me success in contemplation. With every deep breath, I smelled the distinct scent of pine trees. The only sound came from a pair of cardinals. Walking out of the forest, I felt better, much better. Relaxing with nature was an important part of my daily life and I thought about it the first thing in the morning. I received around seventy telephone calls a day in my business and the peace of nature kept me centered. Two years ago I never had time for a twenty-minute break. Now, I looked forward to leaving the office and giving my mind a rest.

I took Hettie's maxim to heart about Less Is More and began to eliminate some of my daily distractions. I used to listen to news on the morning drive into work, but bad news outweighs good news with the media. Now I listened to music and my life had become more peaceful. We can control some of what comes into our life, and I made a constant effort to keep my distractions at a minimum.

After I returned my secretary came into my office and said, "Do you have a minute?"

"Sure Jinny, have a seat."

She sat across from me and said, "Are you studying yoga?"

"Are you kidding me? No, I am not. Do I look more limber?"

"I've been into yoga for years and you have a look in your eyes like people get when they experience the essence of yoga. You've changed this year and for the better. You're calm now. What or who changed you?"

"My friend, Hettie Keller, is responsible. Seeing her on a regular basis has been a soothing experience for me. She's a sage and she has spirit."

Jinny was nearing retirement and she devoted much of her spinster life digging into mine. Her nose was skinny and long. She wore large, thick brown-rimmed glasses that magnified the size of her eyes, and they made her look menacing. However, she was prompt, loyal and brilliant. She was an excellent gatekeeper because she realized the value of time. She made me more effective and productive. That's why I put up with her incessant snooping, which was the reason I had not told her much about my relationship with Hettie.

Her voice had the twang of Tennessee in it. "Arnold, you told me you would take me to meet her someday. When can I go?"

"We'll go, we'll go."

"Okay, I'll wait. Now tell me who Mary Beth Taylor is. Can she see you anytime she wants?"

"Jinny, that's none of your business and she can see me any time except when I'm booked for appointments. If you don't stay out of my personal life, I'm going to send you into early retirement."

"How many times have you threatened to do that?"

She knew by the look on my face when to stop pushing and she stood up and walked toward the door. She was tall and lean and she snapped her head around and said, "Pay attention to that woman!" She slammed the door like she always did when she was mad. I was certain that Hettie was "that woman." I had no doubt Jinny was looking up Mary Beth Taylor in the telephone book to see where she lived.

Ten minutes later she opened the door and said, "Your doctor's office is on line three."

Dr. Murphy's nurse said, "He would like to see you in his office tomorrow afternoon at four o'clock."

It had been eighteen months since my quintuple by-pass surgery. I met with my cardiologist in his office and he discussed the results of my recent angiogram. Dr. Murphy said, "I have some bad news."

Those words were becoming much too frequent. I thought of my father and his rare form of skin cancer. When my cardiologist said the words, "More surgery," I thought, "Did he say more surgery?" I said, "Forgive me Doc; my mind was in another world."

He replied, "Your left anterior descending artery is ninety-percent closed. That is your key artery. If it closes death is immediate."

"What do we do Doctor?"

"We need to schedule you for angioplasty next week. Don't worry. It's a piece of cake compared to your by-pass surgery." He stood from the chair behind his desk and walked over to the sofa. Something told me the worse was yet to come. He motioned for me to join him on the couch. He said, "You have arteriosclerosis which is exacerbated by stress. I want you to get out of the real estate business."

I was shocked. How could I stop? After twenty-five years in commercial real estate I was reaching the peak of my career. I had been climbing the mountain of success for thirty-two years, and finally had reached the point where I could see the top. I thought, "Fifty-six years old and done!"

"What if I only worked a few days a week?"

"Arnold, you can't part time anything. Let me put it to you as plain as I can. You're in a stressful business. If you eliminate the stress, you should be able to live a long life. If you don't, your chances of reaching seventy are minimal. Be here in the hospital next Monday afternoon and we'll operate on Tuesday."

"Doc, I'll need some time to finish the deals I'm working on."

"That is okay. There is a long lead-time in your business. I will give you eighteen months to complete your current business."

We stood. From that moment I don't remember a thing until I wandered into the lobby of the doctor's building at Emory's Crawford Long Hospital. I don't know if I walked down the stairs from his office or rode the elevator. The feeling I had then reminded me of the after effects of a head-on collision with a big linebacker. My knees were wobbly. My vision cloudy. Thoughts scrambled. Uncertain. I leaned against the wall and shook my head.

A male nurse stopped and said, "Sir, are you all right? Do you need some help?"

"Thanks, I was groggy, but I'm okay now."

I saw the front doors and walked toward them with caution. I noticed a closed door with a sign that said, "Chapel." I turned and walked inside. It was a small dark sanctuary with four or five pews on each side. There was no altar. The only light inside came through the three stain glass windows in the front of the chapel. A light beam zeroed in on an opened Bible sitting alone on top of a white table. There was a mahogany kneeler in front of the table. I knelt and closed my eyes. Suddenly, a vision appeared in my mind. Hettie was sitting in her room across from me, and her chin was elevated like it was when she gave me a maxim. She said, "PRAYER ALWAYS WORKS." A feeling of serenity came over me. I prayed, "God, please give me the strength to deal with this."

Then I remembered Hettie's words, "Praying without faith is like trying to make lemonade without lemons."

So, I prayed again, "Dear God, I know you will give me the courage to deal with whatever lies ahead. This problem is not just mine. It is ours. Show me the way." After a few more minutes of prayer I stood and returned to the building's lobby. My head was clear. When I reached the parking lot I thought, "I'm going to the river."

After stopping and buying a bird handbook, I drove to a remote location on the Chattahoochee River ten miles above the park where I took Hettie. There was a large flat rock about fifteen feet from the bank of the river. I hopped from one rock to another and sat on the flat rock in the shallow part of the river. There was no other person within sight. While sitting on the rock, I paged through the bird book until I found a picture of the mockingbird. I thought, "I know this bird. It comes into my backyard. It is always alone and the gray tail stands straight up."

Remembering the day Hettie and I stuck our feet in the Chattahoochee, I took off my shoes and socks and eased my feet into the cold river. I leaned back on the rock and shut my eyes as the water cooled my feet and the sun warmed my face. I felt invigorated when I left.

Dressing for my date with Mary Beth reminded me of how nervous I was on the night of the senior prom. It was a good memory. I graduated in 1956 and it was possibly the greatest musical decade of the twentieth century. Almost everybody danced in the '50s. There were classic songs coming out every week and music of that era was the best. I wish Mary Beth could have seen my cool 1949 Chevy. My prom date's mother did not like it and she put a sheet on the passenger side of the front seat so the seven-year old upholstery would not tarnish her daughter's dress.

Mary Beth lived in the northwest section of Atlanta about forty miles from my house. Full of anxiety I was early so I drove around the neighborhood for fifteen minutes. During the course of my real estate work, I had met with many CEOs and executives of national companies and never felt a single twinge of nervousness, but walking up the driveway to her house I almost tripped over my own feet. I dropped the present I had bought for her which was an elegant pewter watering can with a long, slim, curved spout. Before ringing the doorbell I took a deep breath and exhaled slowly.

When she opened the door and I saw her dressed for a night on the town, it took my breath away. She was beautiful. I had seen her twice at the river in workout clothes and no makeup. She smiled and said, "Welcome, Arnold."

I didn't know whether to shake her hand or do a back flip. Rather than utter something stupid, I handed her the gift wrapped in white paper and said, "Here's something that will keep your flowers smiling."

She took it and we walked into the living room. She sat on one end of the sofa and said, "Please sit down." She pointed to the sofa and I sat at the other end in silence as she unwrapped the present. She pulled out the watering can and said, "What a wonderful gift. Thank you."

I smiled, "You're welcome. I remember you telling me at the river about your flowers."

She stood and looked at me with those gorgeous green eyes and said, "What can I bring you to drink?"

"That's easy. I am a water drinker."

"Why don't you come with me to the kitchen and then we'll sit outside for a few minutes."

I followed her. What a beauty. She had on a black chiffon dress with spaghetti straps. I remembered that when we were at the river and we both had on our running shoes, we were the same height. But tonight with her black sling-back heels she was a couple of inches taller. She had on black stockings that accentuated her attractive legs. The tips of her long blond hair bounced off the center of her back as she walked. The scent of her perfume was enchanting.

We took the drinks outside, and sat in comfortable blue cushioned chairs around a white table on her red brick patio. The early fall evening was flawless under a pale blue sky. A full harvest moon hung low on the horizon. When we started talking it was as if two lifetime friends had been reunited after years of separation. I have never laughed as much as I did that evening. All of our stories were new and together we cherished the discovery of each other's experiences. We were both adventurers who had much in common. We were falling "in like."

After an hour of conversation and laughter Mary Beth said, "What time are our reservations at the Ritz?"

I said, "We're thirty minutes late now, but they will hold them for us until eleven."

She sipped on her white wine and with a twinkle in her eyes asked, "Do you think their customers could handle all of this laughter? I have salmon in the fridge and we could grill outside."

I stood and took off my coat, snatched my tie off and threw them in a vacant chair. "I love your style. Let's eat here."

She stood and said, "You've seen me in running clothes before so I'm going back to the bedroom to change."

"Where's your phone? I'll call the Ritz and cancel our reservations."

We talked and laughed while eating. She played great music and when "Proud Mary" by Credence Clearwater began I said, "How about a dance?"

She winked at me and jumped up. "I love that song."

I remember looking at her and watching her long legs move to the rhythm of the song. The full moon was brilliant over her left shoulder. Her green eyes sparkled. Somehow, I knew that I would never forget that moment and I never have. We danced as if we had been partners all of our lives. Later that evening she served coffee and a homemade chocolate cake that was awesome. The six hours we were together felt more like thirty minutes. When I left her house at one o'clock in the morning we gave each other a short hug, but it was long enough to send chill bumps all over me. It was the best time I've ever had on a first date.

Although the week began in misery, it was ending on a higher note because of my Friday evening with Mary Beth and my upcoming visit with Hettie. As I drove into Atlanta on Saturday morning I thought of how sorrowful Hettie was when she told me about the mockingbird, "I don't think I'll ever hear that song again."

As luck would have it, the day I bought the bird handbook and recognized the mockingbird, I saw it in the backyard. It was perched in a dogwood tree singing away. I kept a tape recorder in my car, so I brought it into the yard, pushed the record button, and placed it under the tree. I taped at least five minutes of the bird singing. I couldn't wait to see the expression on my friend's face when she heard the mockingbird's song.

After spending a few minutes with Carol and catching up with the latest news about her romance with Chucky, I walked into Hettie's room with our meal in hand and the small recorder in my pocket. "Good morning, Hettie."

She was sitting as usual in her chair with the Braille book in her lap. "And good morning back at you. I smelled that chicken when you walked in the front door."

I leaned over and gave her a kiss on the cheek. "Got a surprise for you today."

"What is it? I love your surprises."

I sat the KFC boxes on her bed and reached into my pocket for the recorder. "We're going to have some music with our chicken."

She raised her head toward me and said, "Oh, boy! I can't wait. Hurry up and fix the meal."

I placed a napkin over her lap and set the box with the two drumsticks on it. She reminded me of a little kid, "Go ahead. I'm ready for the music." I sat across from her in the other wingback chair. A few seconds after I pushed the play button, she sprang out of her chair sending drumsticks flying. She yelled, "It's a mockingbird! It's a mockingbird!" She opened her arms wide to me. We hugged each other. She said, "Oh, Arnold! Thank you for letting me hear the mockingbird's song one more time."

"You're welcome."

After retrieving the drumsticks, and washing them off underneath the faucet, we finished our Saturday afternoon picnic in her room. She talked about her childhood and about the property in north Georgia where she spent the first twelve years of her life. We reminisced. We laughed. I brought her a piece of Mary Beth's chocolate cake. Hettie took a bite and said, "Why this is homemade. Who made it for us?"

"Oh, a friend of mine."

"Do you have a girl friend?"

Even though she was ninety-five and thirty-nine years older, Hettie had developed a crush on me. We had grown very close and become a huge part of each other's life. Other than a relative, she had never heard me mention another woman's name. I had decided earlier not to talk to her about Mary Beth. I evaded her question, "Hettie Keller, with you in my life, how in the world would I have the time for another woman?"

She laughed and continued eating her cake. After we finished, I carried the boxes back to the kitchen. Carol was off in another room and I fixed us two cups of coffee to have while we read. Every Saturday, we spent thirty minutes reading to each other. As much as we laughed, cried, and talked together, it was our reading and the discussion of books and authors that was the foundation of our friendship. We drank coffee and sat in the beige wingback chairs with books in our laps. I had surprised her earlier with a footstool so that she would be more comfortable with her feet resting as opposed to dangling above the floor. There were quite a few of my surprises around her room including a talking clock that told you the time in a deep male voice when you pushed the button. Hettie loved to hear that voice and always knew the time.

Despite her age, she had a sharp mind and reading books was her passion. She read a book a week as well as her Bible daily and whatever book we were reading together. She was so proficient in Braille that she could recite the words on a page from the tips of her fingers as fast I could read the same page out loud. We alternated the pages and read back and forth.

Today we were finishing "The Old Man and the Sea" by Ernest Hemingway. She was reading, "Up the road, in his shack,

the old man was sleeping again. He was still sleeping on his…
"What's that word after "his," Arnold?" Hettie always did that to me because one day she had asked me about a word when I had nodded off to sleep. When I awoke in a stupor, she kidded me. From then on I knew at least one time every Saturday she would ask me, "What's that word after…"

"Hettie, I'm not asleep. The word after "his" is "face.""

She laughed and continued, "He was still sleeping on his face and the boy was sitting by him watching him. The old man was dreaming about lions." She closed her Braille book. I closed mine. I took her book and set it among the pile along her wall.

She said, "Don't you love Hemingway? This is my favorite book of his."

"Yes, I do admire his talents. Nobody tells a story better."

"You're a good story teller yourself."

"Thank you, but telling stories and putting them down on paper are two different matters."

Hettie leaned forward in her chair, "You majored in English and Journalism didn't you? You graduated from college so you must have some talent for writing."

"I think I do, but I've never had to do it for a living though."

"Forget doing it for living." She said. "Write for the fun of it."

"Okay, I will. I'll sit down this week and write a short story for you."

"Will you read it to me next Saturday?"

"Yes, but now I'm waiting for today's maxim."

She raised her chin and said, "Maxim Number Five is EDUCATE THE MIND."

"My whole life was changed by education. I'm not talking about just doing schoolwork. Books have been my path for discovery. The whole world is opened to those who read. When I was a child my mother cuddled me in her lap. We sat by the fireplace in a rocking chair and she read stories to me every night. It was listening to those stories in the warm lap of my mother that kindled in me the desire to learn how to read. Thank goodness for my parents and Louis Braille. Together, they changed my life for the better. Many times I have thanked God for giving my parents the foresight to send me to school. Without education I would have been a burden on my family all of my life."

"Hettie, you can read Braille as fast as I can read script."

She smiled, "Thank you. I think I'm ready for my nap now."

"Okay, let me help you." Glancing at my watch, I noticed it was earlier than usual. I thought she looked tired when I first saw her today. I wondered if she was feeling okay. Maybe she was coming down with something.

I helped her out of the chair and onto her bed. I sat beside her and pulled the afghan over her legs. I took her hand in mine. We always spent a few minutes holding hands while saying our last words of the week to each other. There was no small talk today.

Suddenly, Hettie said, "Tell me what happened this week that upset you so?"

I told her about my father's condition with cancer and his prognosis. She nodded and squeezed my hand as I continued to talk about my visit to my cardiologist. I told her that I would have to give up my career in commercial real estate. She said, "Oh, Arnold. Bless your heart. You've had a rough week. Why didn't you tell me about this earlier?"

"Because I didn't want to worry you."

"Arnold, I love you and I'll do anything for you. Besides, there's no need to worry when you have faith in God."

I squeezed her hand, "Thank you, Hettie."

She said, "Now, listen close to what I'm going to tell you. When faced with adversity, always find something to thank God for."

"Okay, I'll try it."

She said, "No! Don't try. Do it. Promise me that when you get home you will thank God for something."

"I promise."

"Good! You be careful driving home. You've got a lot on your mind."

I gave her a hug, a kiss on the cheek, and we said our good-byes. I stood and started walking toward the door.

Just before I left the room she said, "One more thing – tell Mary Beth that her cake was delicious."

I spun around, "No way! How did you know?" I walked to her bed and leaned over, "Please tell me how you knew about Mary Beth?"

"Well, that afternoon we met her on the Chattahoochee River you sounded like a teenager talking when we drove home. I knew you were smitten. Then I never heard anything about her again."

I reached down and held her hand, "So how did you know today?"

She smiled, "Underneath the pain in your voice, I sensed a sound of warmth and cheerfulness that I haven't heard before. When you told me that a friend of yours baked the cake it was the tone in your voice when you used the word, 'friend,' that gave you away. Mary Beth is one lucky woman to have you in her life. Please bring her by to see me again. Will you?"

"I sure will and we'll start another book next week." She squeezed my hand. Driving home, I thought about how weak she looked.

CHAPTER EIGHT

Lying on your back and staring at the hospital ceiling while being pushed on a gurney along an antiseptic smelling corridor is an intimidating experience. I was on my way to the operating room. Mary Beth had hold of one hand and my sister had the other. Rolling down the hospital corridor, I told them, "Everything is going to be fine. My doctor told me this was going to be a piece of cake."

Mary Beth said, "We'll see you back in the room." She leaned down and gave me a kiss on the cheek. It was my first kiss from her.

As the preoperative medication took effect my thoughts drifted back to the days that followed my earlier quintuple by-pass surgery.

The morning after that horrific operation, I had come down with pneumonia and spent eight days in the intensive care unit. With a ventilator in my mouth I couldn't talk. My arms were strapped to the rails of the bed, which prevented me from jerking it out. I had tubes coming out of everywhere and my face was swollen as large as a volleyball. My twenty-one-year old son came to see me the morning after surgery. When he saw me for the first time his jaw dropped, he gasped, and his face was covered with fear. I couldn't say, "Don't worry. I'm going to be fine." Greg leaned down and tried to smile, but instead tears rolled down his cheeks. He cried as he stared at my gray face deprived of oxygen.

He told me later, "Dad, the first time I came to see you in the hospital I knew you were going to die. You looked horrible."

"Son, looks are deceiving – as bad as I looked, I felt worse."

With every breath a struggle, I vowed to give my son some comfort when he came to see me the next afternoon at one o'clock. Before his arrival I motioned with my head for my nurse to come to the bedside. I took a pencil and wrote her a note, "Son coming 1 p.m. Please release hands. Promise won't pull out ventilator." She untied my hands around 12:55 p.m.

Since my son was a child, we had a two thumbs up sign that we gave each other when everything was okay. One Saturday morning when he was eight, I stood on the sidelines watching him play goalie in a soccer game. An opponent closed in on his goal and kicked the ball hard. Greg made an unintentional brilliant stop with his face. He fell to the ground and I rushed onto the field to see if he was all right. When he raised his head I saw that it was covered in blood. The instant he saw me, he gave me the two thumbs up sign.

The ICU had a large round clock on a gray wall over the entrance door. When Greg walked in he looked straight at my bed, probably wondering if I was still alive. As soon as our eyes met, I winked and raised both of my thumbs. With a broad grin, he ran to my bed. He leaned down and kissed me. He cried again, but this time they were tears of relief not fear. "Dad, I couldn't sleep all night from worrying about you."

I handed him a note that said, "Son, I will get better every day." After he left the nurse came over to the bed and refastened my hands. Even though I was pumped full of morphine and remember very little from those days in intensive care, I will never forget my son's grin when he saw my two thumbs up sign.

Like the doctor said, there was no comparison between by-pass surgery and angioplasty. When they brought me back to the hospital room, Mary Beth was there in the chair next to the bed. She had on dark green suit and a white blouse. She had fallen asleep and her beautiful face was serene. I watched her until she woke up. She grinned and said, "Hello, Arnold. Feel like dancing?"

She rose and came over to the bed and took my hand, "Really, how are you feeling?"

"Good, but woozy. Let's dance later."

She sat by the bed and held my hand. We talked for a few minutes and she invited me to dinner at her house on Saturday. When she left the room, I dozed off to sleep. The next afternoon a huge bouquet of flowers were delivered to my room. I opened the card and read these words from Mary Beth:

"Dear Arnold, I picked these flowers from my garden. I hope they brighten your day as much as you have brightened mine. Get well soon and be ready for the best rack of lamb you have ever had on Saturday night. Warm regards, Mary Beth."

Two days later I left the hospital feeling better than I had in a year. With the artery opened my energy level was significantly increased. I thought, "I feel like dancing." I spent a lot of time in front my mirror getting dressed for my date with Mary Beth. I chose black slacks with a white shirt and a long sleeve black cashmere sweater.

When I arrived at her house Mary Beth and Willie greeted me at the front door. She had on navy blue pants with a white turtleneck. We sat on her patio as she went back and forth to the kitchen preparing dinner. We ate in her dining room with candlelight and soft music. Before the meal she reached over for my hand and said, "God, bless my friend, Arnold. Thank you for bringing him to the Chattahoochee River with his friend, Hettie. Bless this food and all of our family. Amen."

Conversation had always been easy for me, but talking with Mary Beth was as natural as breathing. She married like I did right out of college. She had two daughters in the first three years of her marriage. They both lived on the West Coast. Her husband was killed in an automobile accident fifteen years ago. She was an attorney for one of Atlanta's largest law firms and specialized in real estate. We knew a lot of the same people, and the more we talked we realized that we had been to many business and social functions on the same occasion, but had never met each other.

After dinner I helped her with the dishes and we took our coffee into the den. We sat on her sofa and I said, "That was an incredible dinner. You were right. It was the best lamb I've ever had. Where did you learn to cook?"

"Do you remember me telling you about my grandmother in New Mexico?"

"Yes, wasn't it Nettie?"

"That's her. Most of what I cook, I learned from her. When I was a teenager she lived with us for awhile."

She glanced at her watch, and said, "Georgia is playing Tennessee tonight and it's on ESPN. I'm a big Georgia fan. Would you mind if we watched the rest of the game?"

"Of course not, you know I love football."

When she stood up and turned on the television, I thought, "How lucky can a man be? Mary Beth is spiritual, intelligent, witty, a great cook and she likes football." When she saw the score on the screen, Georgia 14 Tennessee 3, she turned to me and said, "Go Georgia! Beat Tennessee!" She took her shoes off, returned to the sofa, and nestled next to me on the couch. After a Georgia victory she said, "Now, do you feel like dancing?"

We walked out to the patio and danced to five or six songs. The last song she played was "Earth Angel" by the Penguins. Holding her in my arms and swaying to the music was a magical feeling. After dancing we returned to her den and drank coffee and talked into the wee hours of the morning. Our conversation was entertaining and enlightening. She asked me, "What's the funniest thing that's ever happened to you?"

"Mary Beth, I've had a lot of them. Let me think about that while I get another cup of coffee. Would you like some more?"

"Heavens no, I'll be up half the night as it is."

When I returned, I told her a funny story:

"A year after my football injury, I decided that I wanted to be priest, so I entered the priesthood. My diocese sent me to a seminary in Lebanon, Kentucky. Most men enter the seminary as soon as they graduate from high school, but since I had three years of college they put me in a group called Special College. There were thirty-five of us living in the dormitory. We had something called grand silence. It meant no one could make a sound or speak to anyone after 9 p.m. If you sneezed you had to muffle it. The wake up alarm sounded at 5:30 in the morning, and the grand silence continued. It was like a fire drill every morning. Our dorm had only three sinks and two toilets for thirty-five guys. We stood silently in line to brush our teeth and shave. Not a word was spoken. The only noise came from the sound of water running or flushing. Even coughs were suppressed. We dressed, put on our long black cassocks and attached the white collar around our necks. We walked in single file to the chapel every morning.

"We looked like a line of penguins marching through a park as we walked to church. There was no talking except for the prayer responses during mass. We walked in silent single file after the service to the cafeteria. When the meal was blessed we could speak, and then a volcano of words erupted. After two months in the seminary I knew that I could never live a life of celibacy. One morning I woke up and thought, 'Other than making a break for it, how can I get out of here today?' Lebanon, Kentucky is a town that is located in the middle of nowhere. I remember thinking, 'I know a bus brought me here from Louisville, but will one take me out?' Standing in the sink line that morning I thought, 'It will take something drastic to get me expelled today.'

"On the morning march to the chapel the perfect opportunity for dismissal presented itself. I had not seen a woman in two months. There she was. She worked as a laundress in a small red brick building about fifty yards off our path. I gave out a wolf whistle that could have been heard in Tennessee. It shocked the silent seminarians so much that the person leading the line stopped and everyone slammed into the seminarian in front of him. The penguin look-a-likes tripped and covered the ground like fallen dominoes. Laughter abounded as we picked ourselves up and continued our march. Later that afternoon I was on a bus to Louisville and a train to Birmingham, my home."

Mary Beth had started laughing when I mentioned the wolf whistle, and she was still laughing when I finished the story. It was two o'clock in the morning when I gave her a hug and left her house. We saw each other at least twice a week for the next three months.

As I continued my weekly meetings with Hettie, I noticed a slow but steady decline in her health and energy. She was still mentally sharp, but she didn't bounce out her chair any more like she did when she heard the mockingbird's song. Because she had always been so vibrant, I was concerned and took her to my doctor for an evaluation.

Dr. Brown said, "She's ninety-six-years old and her parts are wearing out."

On the way back to the home we stopped to eat at Morrison's Cafeteria again, but there was no fun game like we had a few years ago. However, she never lost her love for reading and every week, I wrote her a short story and read it to her. She loved listening to them and encouraged me to continue writing.

"You're a wonderful story teller," she said. "Please keep writing."

"Hettie, most of my Saturday mornings are now spent on the computer working on a story for you."

She reached for my hand and said, "I can't imagine how gloomy these nursing home years would have been without you in my life."

I squeezed her hand and said, "Thank you. We've had some great times. How many brownies do you think we've shared together?"

She laughed, "Over a hundred at least."

I lifted her feet up on the footstool and then sat in my chair. "Hettie, you and Joe were married for thirty-seven years. What do you think is the single most important factor for a successful marriage?"

"Are you having any ideas along those lines?"

Once again her intuition was spot on. "I was curious why you and Joe had such a great relationship."

"The most important element of a strong relationship is communication. Our inability to see each other was a distinct advantage."

"How do you mean?"

"Sighted couples observe looks of all kinds on the face of their partner: disappointment, doubt, and anger, as well as love, hope and glee. Having read thousands of books, I've learned something about body language. There was no such thing for Joe and me. We had to rely totally on our conversation and we learned to choose our words with care. It's not just the words, your tone of voice is important too. People with sight make assumptions as to what their mate is thinking based on how they look. As you know it is impossible to read a person's mind, but couples try to convince themselves that they know the unspoken thoughts of their mate."

"Hettie, you have an uncanny ability to know what's on my mind from the sound of my voice."

"You're right, that's because I've trained myself to really listen when someone is speaking. Fifty percent of communication is listening. Joe and I both were good conversationalists and great listeners. When Joe came home in the afternoon from selling brooms, I could tell from the sound of his voice whether he had a good day or a bad day. However, I always asked him, 'How did you your day go, sweetheart?' Then he would talk about it. Neither of us presumed to know what the other was thinking."

These words from Hettie made a lot of sense, but she wasn't finished.

"Do you remember me telling you the story about our wedding day when we went back to the park bench where we shared a sandwich?"

"Sure I remember it. What a charming story."

"Joe and I made a promise to each other on our wedding day while sitting on that bench. Right before we left to go to our hotel we held each other's hand and I said, 'Joe, I promise I'll never say or do anything to hurt you.' Joe said, 'me too, Hettie.' We never said a word that hurt each other."

I thought, "What a love story."

Hettie raised her chin and said, "There is no better time to give you my sixth maxim. It is COMMUNICATION ENHANCES LIFE. Now, you understand why I talked to you earlier about communication. Also, remember that it is more important to communicate in tough times than when times are going good."

"When you were explaining to me how people assume what their mate is thinking, I realized how many times I had done that in my life. That is one valuable maxim there, and thank you for sharing it with me. You know what? Christmas is around the corner. Please tell me what you'd like for me to give you?"

She smiled, "If you had not asked me I was getting ready to tell you."

"Yeah, you're not shy about telling me what you want."

"It's called good communication, Arnold."

We both laughed and she continued, "I want a harmonica."

"Then a harmonica it will be. I'll bring my family down this year and we could celebrate together."

She said, "Oh, Arnold. That would be so much fun. This is going to be a special Christmas."

I searched for the best harmonica I could find, and on the Christmas afternoon of 1995 most of my family walked into Hettie's room at two o'clock in the afternoon. We all paused in the corridor and we sang as we entered, "We wish you a Merry Christmas. We wish you a Merry Christmas." She was sitting in her chair reading.

I said, "Hettie, please stay seated. You're going to meet the youngest of our family." My first granddaughter was four months old and I said, "Please cradle your arms because I'm going to give you a baby to hold." Her face beamed as I set my granddaughter in her arms.

Hettie said, "Oh, how I love the fragrance of baby powder. What is her name?"

My daughter, Sarah, said, "Her name is Danielle, Mrs. Keller." Sarah walked over to Hettie and leaned down and kissed on her the cheek. "My name is Sarah. Merry Christmas."

Hettie raised her head and said, "Thank you. It's a pleasure meeting you and your daughter. Your dad talks about y'all so often I feel like I know you." She gently held Danielle close to her chest. "Is she asleep or awake?"

"Oh, she's awake," we said in unison.

"She's a good baby," Hettie said, and she rocked Danielle back and forth in her arms. "It's been at least fifty years since I've held a child this young." After Sarah removed Danielle from her arms my son, Greg, walked over and knelt down at the foot of Hettie's chair and introduced himself. Hettie said, "Why you're the champion whitewater kayaker. Do you think I'm too old for you to teach me how to kayak?"

Greg laughed and said, "Mrs. Keller, from what Dad has told us about you, you'll be going over thirty foot waterfalls in no time. He leaned over and said, "It's too cold for kayak lessons today, but I'm going to give you a Christmas kiss." He kissed her on the cheek.

My sister walked up to Hettie and said, "I'm Arnold's sister. My name is Ann."

Hettie blurted out, "But your brother calls you, 'Sissy.' It's a pleasure to meet you, Sissy."

My sister leaned down and gave her a kiss, and wished her a Merry Christmas.

Hettie loved all of the attention she was receiving and she had a smile on her face most of the time when we were there.

My family had heard many stories about the woman who had taught me more about life than anyone I had ever known other than my parents. Hettie was the epitome of those qualities that I admired in people: spiritual, courageous, witty, and intelligent. They hugged Hettie Keller like they had known her all of their lives.

After the family hugs Hettie sat in her chair while we gave her presents, and she had fun opening all the gifts. I saved the harmonica for last. She was excited because she knew it was coming. We sat on her bed watching her tear off the paper and throwing it aside like a child. When she felt the harmonica the expression on her face mirrored her joy. She rose from her chair and placed the instrument to her lips and began to play, "Silent night. Holy night. All is calm." Our family began to sing, "All is bright. Round yon Virgin Mother and Child." Danielle had been taking a nap in the lap of her mother and she woke up with the sound of music. Our singing inspired Hettie and after she finished "Silent Night" she went straight into "Jingle Bells, Jingle Bells." We continued to sing. Mrs. Weldon from next door walked into the room and then one by one the other occupants of the home entered Hettie's room. Before she finished there were twelve people, including Carol, standing in her room and singing Christmas carols.

The more we clapped the straighter Hettie stood. She had studied music at Perkins, and she was in a musical troupe that had played at Atlanta's Fox Theater back in the '40s. Hettie played a medley of tunes that lasted for thirty minutes. After her sterling performance on the harmonica everyone clapped and cheered and wished each other a Merry Christmas. My family had come in separate cars so I could spend some private time with Hettie.

Hettie and I had developed a Christmas tradition of reading out loud together Truman Capote's "A Christmas Memory". I read the story and the role of the narrator, "Buddy," which was Capote, and she read the part of Buddy's elderly niece, "Sook."

Carol brought coffee and her fiancé, Charles, into the room and the four of us sat in Hettie's room and visited for a few minutes. Carol and Charles sat in the chairs and held hands the whole time. Hettie said, "This has been a wonderful day, but all this excitement has tired me. Would you please fix my bed for a nap?" I fluffed the pillow and helped her onto the bed as Carol and her fiancé left the room.

I sat on the edge of the bed and held Hettie's hand.

She said, "Arnold, you have a lovely family. They are considerate and well mannered. I see why you are so proud of them, but I can tell that you are their rock and their strength. Although the role you play in their lives in admirable, you need a rock too. Let me be your rock, will you?"

"You already are. More than you know."

She beckoned with her right forefinger and I leaned my head down. She whispered, "Next to Joe, you're the best friend I've ever had." She kissed me on the cheek and put her arms around my neck and hugged me.

I squeezed her back and said, "I love you, Hettie. Merry Christmas."

She sighed, "I love you too, Arnold. Today was the best Christmas."

CHAPTER NINE

Wise people have a knack for teaching without preaching. That is what Hettie Keller did for me.

Driving into see her on a cold February morning, I realized she began tutoring me the first day we met. When I walked into her room that day, I commented on the huge stacks of Braille books. She told me that those volumes were the foundation of her soul. She didn't make a big deal of it – just stated a fact. After three years of listening to her wisdom I realized that significant changes were evolving in my life – all for the better. Being the classic Type A person, I had spent a life of running fast and hard. Now my heart condition had forced me to slow down. Initially, it was agony. It was Hettie who taught me that slowing down was not a bad thing. She was the personification of patience, peace and happiness.

Born in a cotton field, blind at four months and a student at Harvard in 1927, she had taught many people how to read Braille, and now her teaching was focused on me. Hettie told me about her early years on the farm in the first decade of the twentieth century. A single fireplace in the living room heated the house. In the fall they put sweet potatoes in the embers and brought the cotton stems inside to pick. Those formative years on the farm with her parents were dear to her.

One of my favorite stories she told me was about the two-mule wagon taking the cotton to the gin. Imagine white, soft cotton packed six feet deep inside the wagon's wooden side rails. Her dad would load the wagon and then place the eight-year old Hettie on top of the fluffy crop. She said she sank down and rode all the way to the gin with her parents in front and her dog Sarge trotting behind.

I asked her, "What do you remember about those trips?"

"The warm feeling and the aroma of the soft cotton all around me, the cracking sound of the wooden wheels, Sarge barking at cows and the song of the mockingbird."

"What a great scene. I can picture you surrounded by cotton."

"Arnold, it's the peaceful, simple things in life you remember as you get older."

Her reply of one sentence is something I will never forget. During the first year of our relationship she didn't mention the Harvard education. She was humble, yet proud in a proper understated manner. A few months ago I told her about one of the large office lease transactions that I negotiated. It was a twenty-five million dollar deal. She listened to my story and then said, "Given a choice today, would you prefer another deal like that or seeing your grandchildren graduate from college?"

"I'll take the cap and gown any day."

"Wise choice, young man."

I loved it when she called me "young man." When I arrived Carol had greeted me with a hug and two cups of hot chocolate. "Hettie's feeling somewhat puny today. I can't think of a better way to cheer her up than your visit and a cup hot chocolate."

"Thanks, we'll talk later. I'll go on back and see her."

Walking down the corridor to her room, I saw the Braille book in her lap, but she wasn't reading. She had nodded off to sleep. I stopped at her doorway and wondered if I should let her doze for a few minutes or wake her up. She raised her head, "Do I smell hot chocolate?"

"Yes, Scent Master. We have a treat before we eat."

She smiled, "I'm happy you're here. It's always a good day when you are with me."

I leaned over and gave her a kiss on the cheek. "I'll be right back because I left the chicken in the kitchen."

I turned around and saw Carol coming in our direction with the boxes in hand. She came in and asked, "How are you feeling, Mrs. Keller?"

"Much better now, thanks. I've got Arnold and hot chocolate too."

Carol looked at me and winked.

Feeding Hettie took longer now. She always had a good appetite, but it was almost gone. I had to coax and encourage her to eat as much as she could. We finished our meal and she said, "Tell me what's been happening in your life?"

It had been a rough week for me. Among the few hardships, was the fact that one of my close friends had deceived me. "Hettie, did you ever have a good friend do you wrong?"

"Of course, I have. What happened to you?"

Hettie had a white shawl over her shoulders. She pulled it up around her neck and listened as I told her about one of my friends and how he deceived me. Every so often she raised her chin like she did when she gave me the maxims. She was a good listener. After I finished she said, "Give me your hand."

Since my chair was close enough to feed her, all I had to do was reach out my hand to hers. She held it and said, "Thank you for bringing me into your life and for sharing your disappointments with me."

"Isn't that what good friends do?" I asked.

She smiled and squeezed my hand. "Your friendship means the world to me."

"What should I do about my buddy that lied to me?"

Hettie paused and raised her chin again. "You should forgive him, and let me tell you why. Here is Maxim Number Seven: POWER IN FORGIVENESS. One of the toughest things in our life is to forgive those who have hurt us. It's human nature to carry a grudge against people who have disappointed us, but there is so much peace in forgiving. An angry heart will not allow peace to be with you."

I asked, "What's the old saying? 'I can forgive, but I'll never forget.'"

"Yes, that's what a lot of people say, but you must forget as well. The real purpose of our journey through life is to find peace. You can never have peace burdened by memories of past disappointments. You have to let them go."

"Hettie, that's a lot easier said than done."

"I agree. I've been discriminated against in ways you could never imagine. The handicapped were not treated well in the first half of this century. I've endured many cruel remarks just because I was blind. On occasions I would be walking down Peachtree Street with my guide dog and hear someone yell, 'Get away from me blind woman.' I've been treated as if my blindness was leprosy."

"Tell me how you forgave and forgot?"

"You take it out of your hands and give it to God."

"What's the best way to do that?"

"Whenever I was confronted with a derogatory remark, I said a silent prayer, 'God, give us both strength.' It's difficult to pray for someone and carry a grudge against them too."

"But, Hettie this guy lied to me."

"What he did was deplorable. However, there is real power in the act of forgiveness. Let's say a prayer together for him right now. Join hands with me, please."

I took her hand and listened as she bowed her head, "Father God, we come to You in prayer. Please know that Arnold forgives …" She raised her head toward me and said, "What's his name?"

I told her and she continued, "Please know that Arnold forgives Bill and we ask You to bless them both with Your love and the spirit of forgiveness. Amen."

She lifted her head and said, "Now, you have initiated the process of forgiving and forgetting."

"Do you mean to tell me it is as simple as praying for them?"

"Yes, the power of prayer is a great force and never underestimate its value."

"Okay, I'm not going to start doubting you now."

Suddenly, a pained look appeared on her face. I was alarmed. She gritted her teeth, and said, "Oh! No!"

I jumped up and realized that Hettie had a bowel movement. "Let me get Carol for you." I hurried down the hall and back to the kitchen. No Carol. I called out, "Carol where are you?"

She answered from the back of the house, "I'm in Mrs. Johnson's room."

I ran down the hall and Carol met me in the doorway.

"What's wrong?" Carol said, seeing the troubled look on my face.

"Hettie had a bowel movement and soiled herself."

Carol frowned, "I can't come right now. I have a serious situation with Mrs. Johnson. There are diapers in the top drawer of Hettie's chest. Will you change her for me?"

I was speechless. I had only changed diapers on my children when they were little and that was a long time ago. I didn't even know that Hettie wore diapers. She did not have one on when I helped her at the cemetery. My main concern was for Hettie and her dignity. I knew she was embarrassed. "How long will you be with Mrs. Johnson? "

"She's having difficulty in breathing and I may have to call EMS. It will be awhile before I can get to Hettie."

I had no choice. My friend was in need. "I'll take care of it."

I walked back to her room and she was sitting in her chair. She had a combined look of fright, discomfort and embarrassment. I thought, "Think of something funny to say to her." I entered her room and said, "Carol has an emergency with Mrs. Johnson, and she can't come. I'm going to have to change your diaper, but I want you to know that I will never be back here again."

Hettie laughed because she knew I was kidding. She said, "Let's get Saint Peter to close that curtain too. Joe doesn't need to see this."

We walked into her bathroom. I got washcloths and towels and cleaned her up. I took a dress from her closet and put it on her. We returned to her room and she said, "Thank you for taking care of me."

"You're welcome. Are you ready for the story I wrote for you last night?"

Her face lit up. "Yes and I would like to lie in bed while you read it."

I helped her onto the bed and tucked the afghan around her legs. She smiled as I began to read:

"Young, red-headed Casey, walked to school every week day because that was the only way he could get there. It was a hard trek through the darkness and he jumped off of his back porch every morning at 5:30. His lunch was in a small sack tied to pole and slung over his shoulder. Today, he had two apples and a piece of hoecake his grandmother made last night. The first mountain Casey had to climb was Wilson's Point. There was no path to follow except his path and he knew every tree and rock on his journey. It was his tenth and final year in school. Everyone was talking about the war and he pretended Germans were hiding behind the loblolly pines. Casey crouched down ever so often and played like his pole was a rifle. 'Pow! Pow!' He yelled for none to hear except the birds and animals of Northwest Georgia. Two hours later he arrived at the one room schoolhouse where Mrs. Pursiful taught all grades one through ten.

'Hey, Red. Guess what?' His fourteen-year-old friend, Floyd, asked when he walked onto the schoolyard.

'What, Floyd?'

'We have a new student. She's a blonde, and almost as tall as you are.'

"When Casey opened the oak door of the school, he saw her. She had on a blue dress and carried a tapestry purse.

"Mrs. Pursiful said, 'Casey, this is Sadie and she's in your grade.'

"Sadie held her hand out to Casey. He shook it, but it was hard to let go. She was the most beautiful person he had ever seen.

'It's good to meet you,' she said.

"Casey nodded his head but found it hard to speak. Mrs. Pursiful placed Sadie in the desk in front of him. When he took a deep breath, she smelled like a spring morning at dawn. They broke for lunch and he got up the nerve to ask her if she wanted an apple. She said, 'Mama always sends me to school with one, but thanks anyway.'

"They sat next to each other on the front steps.

"Floyd stared at both of them while they ate lunch and talked. When Casey stood he reached his hand down and helped her up. She smiled and his knees buckled. The rest of the afternoon was a blur for Casey as he was in a world unknown. He fell lock, stock and barrel in love with Sadie on that September day.

"Two years later they would marry, and soon Casey was called to war. He'd been hunting all his life so it was no surprise to him that he was the best shot in the platoon. However, that meant he ended up on the front lines against the Germans on the plateau forest of the Ardennes in Northeast France. The trees were not as tall as the ones in Georgia, but they were broader. Casey and his platoon were stalking through the snow in search of a German patrol. It reminded him of those walks over Wilson's Point in the winter. The peaceful snow in France was a disaster in disguise for all hell broke loose and bullets came zinging through the air. Casey watched in horror as the German sharpshooters picked off his buddies one by one. After days of fighting only three soldiers were alive in his platoon. He had one apple left that Sadie had sent. He sat behind a tree and shared it with his buddies. It was cold. He was sure that the freezing weather and not fear caused his teeth to chatter. Casey had never been afraid. When he finished eating, he rose and searched for the enemy. He thought he saw something move. A German soldier stepped out from behind a tree and fired his rifle. Casey never heard the 'Pow! Pow!' His final thought was of the girl standing in the school house wearing a blue dress and carrying a tapestry purse."

Hettie said, "I loved that story, even though it had a sad ending. I think you have found a new career for yourself at the young age of fifty-seven."

I thought, "She really does think of fifty-seven as being young."

"The more you write the better you'll get. How long did you work on it?"

"Probably about two hours."

She raised her chin slightly and said, "How many words does the story have?"

"I'm not sure. Let me count them for you." I looked over the story and said, "It appears to be around six hundred words."

She leaned back in her chair, "Have you read the biography of Ernest Hemingway by Carlos Baker?"

"No, have you read it? I thought you didn't like nonfiction."

"You convinced me to try it and since we had been reading Hemingway, I ordered it and read the book last week. How many words do you think Hemingway wrote on an average day?"

"I don't know."

"Take a guess."

"I'll say about a thousand words."

She leaned forward in her chair and said, "Only half of that. Five hundred words a day was a good day for him. Do you know what he said was the most important thing for a writer?"

"What?"

"Write every day. Go to work on time. I learned something else about writing, but first let me ask you a question. When you write a short story for me what is the hardest part of the process?"

"That's easy. The toughest part is writing the first sentence and then the first paragraph."

Hettie smiled and said, "Hemingway had an answer for that dilemma. He overcame that by stopping his work for the day in mid-sentence."

I nodded my head as if she could see me. Sometimes I had to remind myself that she was blind. "Thank you, that's great to know. I can see the benefit of getting started each day by completing the sentence. I've had several courses in journalism and I never heard that useful tidbit. Are you grooming me to be a writer?"

"You're real estate career is almost over and you are way too young to stop working. Can you think of something you'd love to do more than writing?"

I thought about what she said, "No, writing is my first choice."

She smiled, "One more thing, you complement me on my skill in reading Braille, but I have almost ninety years of practice. The more I read the better I become and I'm sure the same holds true for writing. Promise me you'll continue to write."

"I promise."

She reached for my hand and squeezed it, "Did we eat our dessert?"

I had left the two pieces of pie in the refrigerator and I said, "We still have dessert. I'll go get it."

When I returned she said, "Great, key lime pie is one of my favorites."

I smiled and sat on the edge of her bed and fed her. The combination of reading my story, discussing writing and eating dessert took her mind away from the embarrassment she had suffered earlier.

Hettie said, "This has been one of our best days together."

"Why do you think so?"

"You read me your story, you shared your disappointments with me, and you showed me how much you love me. How long has it been since you changed a diaper?"

"Twenty-five years at least and I hope it's twice that before I do it again."

She laughed. "I feel so close to you and that helped me get through an embarrassing situation. You're my best friend and almost like family to me. I miss my family. My brother was young when he died."

"How old was he?"

"He was forty. Charlie was eight years younger than I. He was at the prison in Reidsville and had a fatal heart attack on the day they released him."

"What was he there for?"

"Alcohol was his downfall. He was a great guy until he drank too much and then he got mean. He and four others were fighting in a bar and someone got hurt. My father died first in the 30s, Charlie died in 1947 and momma died a few years later. Momma told me Charlie's eyes became infected just like mine when he was a few months old, but she was able to help him."

I was puzzled, but waited for her to continue.

"You remember me telling you about the infection I got in my eyes when I was four-months old."

"Yes, I do."

"A neighbor told my momma that if she got the bark of a sassafras root, boiled it down, let it cool and then spread it over my eyes it would cure the infection. However, momma got sick with pneumonia and wasn't able to try the remedy on me. Later, when Charlie got the same infection she used the sassafras treatment on him and it worked. He kept his sight."

I shuddered at the thought of how fate had affected Hettie's life and yet she had no bitterness.

"Ever since Joe died in 1975, I've been without family, at least a human family. You know I always considered my guide dogs as part of my family. But now I have you."

"Let me give you a big hug, Hettie." I put my arms around her and held her tight. We said our goodbyes and I stopped in the kitchen to see Carol on the way out.

"How is Mrs. Johnson doing?"

"She's better now. How did your diaper changing go?"

"No problem."

"Arnold, Hettie is getting weaker, and it's harder to dress her for your Saturday visits."

"Please don't dress her for me. What does she wear when I'm not here?"

"Her nightgown and a bathrobe."

"Well, please leave that on her for my Saturday visits."

"It's Hettie insistence to look good for you."

"I'll walk back and talk to her about it." Hettie was asleep and I returned to Carol. "I'll call her and ask her to please not get dressed for me. How is she doing overall?"

"Her appetite isn't very good, and she's losing strength. However, her mind is sharp and all of her vitals are good. Her blood pressure is on the low side, but not in a danger zone."

"Please call me if you think a doctor needs to see her, and I will take her to his office.

"You know I will, and thanks for all you've done for her."

"You're welcome. Now, tell me about Chucky."

"We've arranged for a wedding date."

"Congratulations. That's terrific. When?"

"September the fifth. We would have never met unless you stopped to look in Hettie's window."

I laughed, "I'll never forget that day."

"Chucky and I still laugh about that afternoon too."

Driving home I thought about Hettie and the impact of her wisdom on my life, but the maxim she gave me today would be the toughest one to practice: POWER IN FORGIVENESS. How do you forgive someone when they hurt you? I thought about my friend and how much anguish he caused. I said a short prayer for him.

The car phone rang. It was Mary Beth. "Hi, darling. How's Mrs. Keller doing?"

"She's not as spry as she used to be, and I see her failing."

"How old is she?"

"She'll be ninety-seven in July."

"She's enjoyed a long life. Speaking of long, how long has it been since we've been together?"

"Didn't we go to the movies on Thursday night? So it's been almost forty-eight hours, honey. What would you like to do this evening?"

"It's too cold to go out. Why don't you come over and we'll sit in front of fire place and have dinner. Then I'll whip you in a game of Scrabble."

"Tell me who won the last game?"

She paused and said, "Tell me who had the luck to draw the X, the Z and the J?"

"That would be the winner. Me."

"Just hurry over. I miss you."

"I miss you too, Mary Beth. See you soon."

Whether it was seeing Hettie, talking to Mary Beth, or saying the prayer for my friend, I felt like the title of an Eagle's Song. I had a "Peaceful Easy Feeling."

CHAPTER TEN

Over the next few months Hettie's health declined. I was surprised one Saturday to see an oxygen tank beside her bed. She told me it was used to help her breathe at night. She sensed my concern and assured me that it was nothing to worry about, but she did not tell me about her pneumonia.

My secretary, Jinny, had been persistent in asking to meet Hettie. Even though her favorite hobby was trying to keep track of my personal life, she was a valuable employee and we shared a mutual respect for each other. We left the office together on Friday after lunch and drove to see her. Jinny said, "How are you coming on the deal for the twenty- first floor of the building?"

"I'm close."

Jinny said, "You are always close. I cannot remember you saying, 'I don't have a chance to make this deal.' How long have I worked for you?"

Keeping my eyes on Atlanta's busy expressway I looked straight ahead and said, "Too long."

"What do you mean too long? Without me you would be selling ice on the North Pole."

I laughed. There was a break in the traffic ahead and I glanced over at her for a second and said, "You're right. You have been a great help to me and my career."

She said, "I love the way we kid around with each other and I want you to know you're the best boss I've ever had. You make work fun. I'll never forget the day you had us tossing a coin for twelve hundred dollars. I was so glad that Steve won the money."

I remembered. The commercial real estate business is a roller coaster ride. In good times, it can be lucrative, but in bad times it can be brutal for people working on commission. I had a staff of ten people in the Atlanta office of a national real estate developer and brokerage firm. We had six sales people, a property manager and a support staff of three. During the early 90s the office building market was flat and times were hard for anyone working on commission. I rented a small space in the downtown office building we were leasing and my share of the commission was twelve hundred dollars. I called Jinny and asked her to let everyone know there would be a meeting in our conference room at four o'clock that Friday afternoon. I stopped by my bank and withdrew twelve hundred dollars. I asked the cashier for Benjamins. I had ten pennies in my pocket to use for the game.

When you go through tough financial times it can demoralize an office. None of us had a made a deal in four months and I wanted to do something to boost the spirit and attitude of our employees. I entered the conference room at four and everyone was seated, a few had puzzled looks on their faces because they knew sales meetings were rare for me. Sitting at the head of the table I said, "I'm sorry to inform you…" and then I paused. I could feel the tension from our nervous employees. I reached into my pocket and spread the twelve one hundred dollar bills on the table, and said, "In three minutes one of you will win this money." The expression on their faces changed completely and you could feel the excitement in the room.

I said, "The game is called Pitch and Toss. Everyone please stand and join me on this side of the conference table." I stood and we all lined up along the table about eight feet away from the wall. "The object of the game is to toss these pennies over the table and the coin closest to the wall wins the money."

"Are you playing too?," asked Jinny.

"Absolutely, I practiced this for three hours last night after everyone left the office."

All laughed, because they knew the last thing in the world I would do is waste three hours tossing a coin. "I'll go first so you know what you have to beat." My coin landed about two inches from the baseboard and several people groaned. Rhett asked, "Did you really practice last night?"

"Of course not, that was a lucky toss." This was a game I did not want to win. One by one they tossed the penny over the mahogany table and with only one player left my coin was still the closest. Steve Nagrom had the remaining toss. He was our youngest employee and his wife was expecting in two months. His penny sailed over the table and nestled on the wall like a leaner in horseshoes. He jumped and yelled, "All Righhhhhhht!" He was a happy guy when he left the office an hour later. The next Monday the atmosphere in our office was completely different. There was a presence of enthusiasm and smiles that I had not seen in awhile.

We pulled into the nursing home driveway and I looked at Jinny and said, "When I talked to Carol on the telephone this morning she told me Hettie was felling puny. Let's stay just for a few minutes."

Jinny reached in her bag and brought out a wrapped gift, "I brought her a surprise."

Carol met us at the front door and we talked with her for a few minutes before going to see Hettie. She had a dress on for the occasion, but she did not get up when we entered. "Jinny Williams, meet my good friend, Hettie Keller."

Jinny said, "What a pleasure to meet you, Arnold talks about you all the time."

Hettie raised her chin slightly, "Did he tell you what my favorite cake was?"

I glanced at Jinny, and she said, "Coconut."

"Miss Jinny, let's hug." Hettie spread her arms and Jinny hugged her.

Carol had placed an extra chair in the room and we sat down. "Jinny, Arnold has promised me he would bring you to see me. Thank you for taking time away from your work to come."

"Hey, it is my pleasure. We can't stay long today and I want to give you a small gift." She placed it in her lap and Hettie grabbed it and ripped the paper off. It was a beautiful piece of amethyst shaped like a chapel. It was about the size of a softball. The inside glowed with dark purple. Hettie ran her fingers over the piece as Jinny described it to her. Hettie was so appreciative and she thanked Jinny several times. She loved surprises and I thought, "The wonder of an unexpected gift is always a joy. I made a mental note to give my daughter and son a surprise."

Carol came in and next thing I knew they were talking about wedding plans and I eased out to my car where I had a phone. After twenty minutes of business, I went back to her room. Carol had left and they were talking about the maxims when I entered the room. Jinny said, "Your maxims have really made a difference in my life. My boss has taught me the value of relaxing with nature. He's gives me forty-five minutes every day to be away from the office."

"Has it helped?"

"Mrs. Keller, that is the best part of my day. I've been into yoga for years and the experience I gain in nature is similar to the practice of yoga. Our business is hectic all day, every day. When I awake in the morning, I begin to think about relaxing with nature."

"Since your offices are in the city, where do you go?"

"The Atlanta Water Works is downtown and I have found a neat spot where water birds abound. It only takes a few minutes to drive over there and my mind is refreshed and cleared on the way back. That is one of my favorite maxims."

"When did he give you the maxims?"

"He gave them to me after I saw the differences they were making in his life. I asked him about his personality change and the reason for them, and he told me how your influence had altered his thinking about several important matters in his life."

I entered the room and said, "Okay, that's enough about me. Jinny, we need to leave and get back to the office. I have a proposal that must be in the mail this afternoon." We said our good-byes and Hettie said, "Will I see you again tomorrow, Arnold?"

"Of course, I'll be here around noon."

On the way back to the office Jinny said, "She's the spitting image of the person you talked about. She has such a great outlook. Imagine, living ninety-seven years in darkness?"

I replied, "All those years of being blessed. That's the way she describes her blindness."

Jinny shook her head and muttered, "Remarkable."

As soon as we reached the office, Jinny came in and sat on the sofa while I dictated our proposal. "We need it sent by courier so they will have it today. Thank you."

"You are welcome and thank you for taking me to meet Mrs. Keller."

The next day Hettie and I talked about one of our favorite subjects, baseball. Joe introduced her to the game shortly after they were married in 1938. They listened to the Atlanta Cracker minor league team on the radio every night during the season. Joe took Hettie to Ponce de Leon Park right after they bought a home in the Grant Park neighborhood.

They decided to take in a ball game and arrived at the stadium two hours before it started. They were standing outside when the owner of the team, Earl Manning, came up and asked them, "Have you been to a Cracker game before?"

Hettie said, "We've listened to them for years and Country Brown is my favorite player, but this is our first time at the park."

Earl said, "How about the guide dog? Is he trained to hold it until he gets outside?"

Hettie said, "The dog is trained to go at specific times. I can assure you that will not be a problem."

"The owner took us inside and led us down the aisle. He gave us two permanent seats for every home game near first base. He said, 'There's a family of four with two teenage boys right across the aisle from you. The boys bring their gloves and they can catch a foul ball headed your way."

Hettie said, "Joe and I never thought about the possibility of being hit with a foul ball."

I said, "So how did you like being at the games instead of listening to them?"

"We loved it. There was no better way to spend a summer night than being at the ballpark. The owner told us we could bring our boiled peanuts to the game. The smell of popcorn, hot dogs, cotton candy and fresh mowed grass filled the air. We relished the sounds and the smells of Ponce de Leon Park. We got to know the people around us and they told us whether the batter hit a single, a double or a triple. We learned to recognize a home run from the crack of the bat. We were so close to first base that we could determine by sound whether the runner was safe or out on a close play."

"How could you tell?"

"There are two different sounds: the runner's foot hitting first base and the thrown ball hitting the first baseman's glove. We listened for which came first."

"That's awesome."

"We became quite a sight because over the years we saved Atlanta Cracker paraphernalia. Joe and I both wore the Cracker baseball caps and shirts. One of the fans made a special vest for my guide dog to wear to the game. She had sewn 'Number One Fan' on it. Going to the game became the highlight of our summer days and every one of our guide dogs as well. If we were a few minutes late in leaving the house, our dog barked to let us know it was time to go to the park."

"Where did your dog sit at the game?"

"Beside me. My seat was the first one on the aisle and Joe taught Sarge and our other dogs to stand up on their hind legs when a Cracker hit a home run."

"When the Cracker games stopped after the Braves came to Atlanta in 1966 did you go to the major league games too?"

"No, but we listened to every one of them. I remember Milo Hamilton making the call of Henry Aaron's seven-hundred-fifteenth home run in April of 1974."

"I was at that game."

"Then that was the first time I heard your voice because we heard everyone screaming after Henry hit the homer. Joe died the next year and I never listened to another game but once."

"Why did you stop?"

"It was too painful. Baseball and Joe Keller went together for me, and when Joe passed I gave up the game, but I never forgot the crack of the bat when Eddie Mathews hit a home run. It had a different sound from all the others we heard. He had a big career in the big leagues. Didn't he?"

"Yes, he hit five-hundred-twelve home runs over his major league career. Did you know that Eddie Mathews was the only player to play for the Boston Braves, the Milwaukee Braves and the Atlanta Braves?"

"Hettie said, "No, I did not. What a great piece of trivia. I can't wait to ask Carol that question."

"I had no idea Carol was into baseball."

"She did not know a thing about it until she met Chuck and now she loves the game."

Hettie and I talked about baseball and books for a long time that afternoon. Later she said, "Are you ready for Maxim Number Eight?"

"Yes, I'm always ready to hear your maxims."

She leaned back in her chair and lifted her chin, "Maxim Number Eight is REGULAR EXERCISE IMPROVES. I have no doubt the single most important factor of my long life has been a regimen of daily exercise."

Hettie told me after she received her first guide dog in the forties that she and Joe began to walk five to six miles a day. They walked or took public transportation everywhere they went. Their walk to the ballpark was a roundtrip of five miles. Besides walking, she did a routine of stretching exercises and light weight training every day.

"I've seen you do your stretching exercises. What kind of weight training did you do?"

"You're an athlete, so you will understand. With two-pound weights I did thirty curls every day for my arms. Of course, that was when I was a youngster like you. A year ago, I was down to only five a day, but now I'm too weak to do any."

"What other exercises did you do?"

"I'd lie in bed and tighten up my thigh muscles for five seconds and then relax. I used to do fifty of those every day, but now I only have the strength for five. Strong thighs will prevent knee problems as you get older."

"When you stretch, what muscles do you work on?"

"I stretched my back by reaching to the floor and then I stretched my neck muscles by turning my head side to side while keeping my shoulders straight. Then I tilt my head up toward the ceiling and down to the floor. Stretching helps your mobility. It's important to work the muscles of your arms, legs, back and neck. When you are young – you really should do these so that the quality of your life is better as the years go by."

"You haven't been able to walk much since you've been in the home, have you?"

"I've walked these corridors so many times that I know exactly how many steps it is to each turn, but you're right, my walking has diminished since I came here. I've slowed down a lot in the last year."

"Hettie, you're going to be ninety-seven in six weeks. It's time to slow down don't you think?"

She smiled and said, "Remember, the benefit of exercise is not just for today – it's for all those tomorrows. Do you walk every day?"

"I walk about twenty-five miles a week and I love it."

Hettie said, "Good, every step you take today is a hobble you eliminate in your later years."

I thought, "What a great statement for the value of exercise."

"Would you please help me into bed? I'm tired."

After pulling her spread back and fluffing her pillow, I helped Hettie to the bed. We held hands and talked for a few minutes. I gave her a hug and told her I loved her.

She said, "I love you more than you will ever know."

On the way home, I called Mary Beth from the car, "Hey sweetheart. I've just left the nursing home."

"How's dear Hettie?"

"I'm alarmed. She's got oxygen beside her bed to help her breathe at night."

"I don't think it's uncommon for someone her age to use oxygen," Mary Beth said in a comforting manner.

"You're right, honey. What would you like to do tonight?"

Mary Beth said, "Let's go to the Braves game. A client gave me great tickets close to the Atlanta dugout."

"What a coincidence, that sounds like fun. Hettie and I have been talking about baseball this afternoon. I'll pick you up at 6:30."

On the way home I thought about Hettie and Joe sitting in Ponce de Leon Park with their Atlanta caps and jerseys on. I could picture them both standing with their dog and cheering an Atlanta Cracker home run. Hettie's love for Joe and how they both put each other first in their lives was a classic lesson in love. I wondered if I would be able to do the same thing with Mary Beth someday. I thought, "Will I ever have the opportunity?"

Mary Beth was radiant in her yellow pants and white turtleneck. We talked about my visit with Hettie on the way to the ballpark.

Mary Beth said, "Can't you see that dog with the vest sitting next to Hettie and standing when a home run was hit? What a generous offer the owner made to give them season tickets every year?"

"Tell me about it. Have you ever sat in these seats we have for tonight?"

"No, but other people from our firm have and they said you are almost on top of first base."

We entered Atlanta Fulton County Stadium and sure enough the seats were in the first row about sixty feet from first base. While Mary Beth went to the restroom I closed my eyes and took a deep breath. Immediately I inhaled the summer aroma of cut grass. The world champion Atlanta Braves were playing their archrival the Los Angeles Dodgers. The game was high scoring and Mary Beth was as enthusiastic about the Braves as she was about the Georgia Bulldogs. She jumped out of her seat and yelled at the umpires several times, "You need glasses!" Every base hit by the Braves was greeted with her applause and cheers.

Once, on a ground ball to the shortstop, I closed my eyes and tried to distinguish the sound of the ball hitting the glove and runner's foot hitting first base. I heard the ball smack into the first baseman's glove, but I couldn't hear the sound of the foot slamming on the bag. There was something special about living in Hettie's world even if only for a few moments. I paid close attention to the sound of the bat hitting the ball, but no one hit a home run until our star, Chipper Jones, came to the plate in the seventh inning with the bases loaded. The crowd stood, I closed my eyes and on the first pitch I heard a clear and resounding crack. The crowd roared and I opened my eyes in time to see the ball sail over the center field fence. Mary Beth turned and gave me a high five. Once again, I thought of Hettie and Joe standing and cheering for a homer they couldn't see. The Braves won and while we drove back to Mary Beth's home I told her how Hettie and Joe always put each other first.

She said, "I don't know if I could do that since I've been alone so long. Could you?"

I looked at her and said, "I'm not sure, but I think it might become second nature if I were in love."

The expression in her eyes was something I hadn't seen before, but I had to get mine back on the road. The look on her face confused me. To make matters worse she stopped talking and changed the radio station from the post game wrap-up to a music station. Our relationship had grown, but it was mostly centered on fun and laughter. We had never talked seriously about anything further. Her silence was a sharp contrast to her laughter earlier. Finally, she said, "It's a beautiful night. Why don't we sit on the patio and have some coffee when we get home? There's something I want to tell you."

It was difficult for me to speak because those words, "There's something I want to tell you," almost always spelled trouble for me. With some effort I managed to say, "Sounds good."

The short trip to her house seemed like forever. I had no idea what to expect. The wide swing in my emotions from our great time at the game to a tense situation in the car was almost overwhelming. Mary Beth and I had laughed so much together and we shared many of the same interests. All of our friends thought we were a perfect match. So did I, but I wondered if it was coming to an end.

We arrived at her home and I stepped out of the car to walk around and open the door for her. Before I got there, she opened the door and walked to the house in front of me. If she was trying to send me negative signal, it was working. We entered the house and she said, "Have a seat on the patio and I'll be out soon."

I was confused. I sat on the patio and waited for her to fix the coffee as I petted Willie. She brought it out and she sat in the chair across the table from me. She had always sat next to me. Mary Beth interrupted my thoughts.

"Arnold, I've been in love with you for sometime now." Oh, the joy I felt, but from the look in her eyes I knew this was no time for celebration. Her next words explained her facial expression. "Falling in love with you frightens me."

I took a deep breath.

She sipped on her coffee. Even though I was sitting down, my knees were shaking. Suddenly, I knew how much I loved her, and the thought of losing her was unthinkable.

She continued, "You're everything I ever wanted in a man and you are the most generous person I've ever known. What you have done for Hettie is one of the greatest examples of love that I have ever seen."

I looked at her and wondered what was coming next. Everything sounded good, but the mood was not cheerful. I noticed my hands trembled when I tried to drink the coffee. I never had that experience before.

Tears appeared in Mary Beth's eyes. I gave her a handkerchief and she wiped her green eyes and said, "When I lost my husband fifteen-years ago it almost killed me. There were times when I thought about taking my life and I probably would have if it were not for my daughters."

We had a few conversations earlier about her relationship with her husband, and I knew that she had loved him, still loved him.

She continued, "I'm afraid of losing you. You've had three heart attacks and two heart operations. I realize that you have changed your life style, but you have severe coronary artery disease. You're the first thing I think of in the morning and your smile is with me on my pillow at night. I don't know if I could handle another sudden death, and because of that I'm afraid for us to go forward."

She started crying. I stood up and walked toward her. She stopped me. "Please don't hold me. I love you. I can't resist your arms around me."

I sat back in my chair and picked up the cup of coffee. Steady hands this time.

She said, "Okay, thanks for listening to me. Now, tell me what you think."

"Mary Beth, I love you too. We've talked about our lives and I know you love adventure as much as I do. How can you turn your back on all the love and excitement ahead of us? There are no guarantees in life. A beer truck could run you over in downtown Atlanta tomorrow. How do you know that I might be the one to have to survive without you?"

She looked at me and mumbled, "Please give me some time to think about it."

"How much time do you need?"

She shook her head, "I don't know but at least three months."

I stood, "Mary Beth, I've been waiting for years to meet the right person to spend the rest of my days with. I'm not going anywhere. When you reach your decision you can call me. Can I give you a hug?"

She nodded her approval and I walked over and held her briefly in my arms. She whispered, "I'll call you."

I said, "I'm waiting." I let go and walked away.

CHAPTER ELEVEN

The next time I saw Hettie she was still using oxygen, but she had more bounce and energy than I had seen in the last month. After our lunch she was anxious to finish our current book, "The Yearling." She was excited when she learned that I had brought coconut cake for dessert.

When we read the last page, she closed her book and I stacked it on top of the others along the wall. She said, "I can't wait to give you my next maxim."

"Go right ahead then."

She smiled and crossed her feet on her footstool. She had on a pink cotton nightgown and her bathrobe lay at the foot of her bed. "Please forgive me for not dressing like a lady for you."

"No problem, I want you to be comfortable."

Every time she gave me a maxim, I anticipated the slight raise of her chin and it happened again. "Today's maxim reminds me of you. This is one of my favorites."

"I cherish all of your maxims."

"All right then, Maxim Number Nine is LOVE THY NEIGHBOR," she said. "I feel like I should sit back and listen to you explain this one to me."

"Why me? I love the anecdotes you give me with your maxims."

"You have lived this maxim with me for the past four years. You came to see a total stranger and you have loved me like I was a member of your family. You have given me the most valuable thing you have and that is your time. You've brought total joy into my life. When it comes to this maxim, I have learned from you. There is no greater love for your neighbor than what you have given me. Why you even changed my diaper." She began to cry. I reached over and held her hand. "Please know that these are tears of joy, not sadness," she said. "Arnold, please tell me what LOVE THY NEIGHBOR has meant for you as it relates to me?"

"Hettie, my greatest thrill has come from loving you. I love to hear you laugh, and we've had so many good times. We've read countless books together, and we must have eaten every dessert in the world."

She giggled and said, "Has your life changed since you began to see me?"

"Absolutely!"

"How?"

I scratched my chin and thought about her question. "Well, every time I've done something good for you, my life was blessed."

She interrupted and asked me to help her to put on her bathrobe. I helped her out of the chair and got the navy blue cotton robe and put it on her. I helped her into the chair and she leaned back. I propped her feet on the footstool. She looked as content as I had ever seen her. Although the pink color was gone from her face, there was peacefulness about her that was evident. She smiled and said, "Thank you, and please continue."

"As I said, on every occasion that I did something good for you, my life was blessed."

"Please, give me some examples."

"I remember the first time you asked me to help you find your teeth. I had never held another person's dentures before. After searching for a few minutes, I saw them on the floor under the bed and I thought, 'Maybe, I'll tell her I can't find them.' Instead, I reached down and picked them up and said, 'Here they are. Let me go wash them for you.'"

She giggled. "You had never touched false teeth before?"

"No, that was a first. When I got home that afternoon, my daughter called to tell me she was pregnant and my first grandchild was on the way. When I jumped for joy, I thought about washing your teeth earlier in the day." I thought, "Good begets good."

"You said a mouthful there. Do you have any more examples?"

"Yes of course, the day I changed your diaper."

Hettie said, "How could I forget? I was so embarrassed, but you were such a gentleman in the way you handled the situation you made me feel at ease. What a demonstration of love for your neighbor. Did something good happen to you after that?"

"Oh, yes. The next day I received some good news about my father. The doctors decided not to amputate his arm."

Hettie leaned forward in her chair and said, "My prayers are with your dad, how is he doing?"

"He's not any better, but he's not much worse."

She said, "In my opinion the love of our neighbor is our highest calling, the greatest of all earthly acts, and it is one that God rewards with abundance. You have an easy way with people. I bet that you have never met a stranger. Use that talent to help others. The world is full of individuals who do not have your people skills. They are shy and withdrawn. When they muster the courage to help their neighbor in some small way God will bless them tenfold."

"I have learned so much from you, Hettie. Do you feel like a cup hot chocolate?"

She grinned, "With marshmallows."

She was asleep when I returned, but the aroma woke her and she said, "This has been a meaningful day. I'm glad we finished another book. Aren't you?"

"Yes, I would have never read "The Yearling" without your recommendation and the wisdom of your maxims have really made a difference in my life."

"Your blessings have come from God. You have loved your neighbor and God has rewarded you."

We drank hot chocolate and talked for another thirty minutes. Then Hettie asked me to help her into bed. I got her tucked in and nestled the afghan over her legs. We held hands as usual and talked some more.

She said, "Arnold, I don't have long now. The pneumonia is worse."

I was stunned. It was hard for me to comprehend what she said. No one had told me she had pneumonia. I did not have a clue that she was that sick. A lump welled up my throat and it was all I could do to say, "I sure am going to miss you." After a short pause, I regained my composure and I said, "Please do me a favor."

She replied, "I'll do anything I can for you."

"Okay, when you get to Heaven, please help me get there."

She wiggled her right forefinger, as usual that meant she wanted me to lean down and hear what she had to say. I dropped my head down closer to her and listened as she whispered, "Who do you think I am, Houdini?"

We both burst out laughing. We held each other's hand and neither of us could stop laughing until she said, "Of course, I will help you."

I squeezed her hand and said, "Thanks, I sure will need it." She beckoned with her finger again and I leaned toward her. She said, "Please do me a favor."

Without hesitation I said, "I'll do anything for you."

Hettie said, "Write a story about us. Please tell others about all the fun we had and be sure to include the afternoon you played the game with me in Morrison's Cafeteria. Also, tell them about my maxims and how they will improve the quality of our life on earth. Will you do that for me?"

"I sure will."

"After you finish the story I want you to have it published."

"Writing a story is one thing, having it published is another. I have a friend who wrote a novel and he tried to get it published. He told me it was easier to win the Georgia Lottery than finding a publisher for a first time author."

She raised her chin and said, "Do you remember what I told you about passion and how you can walk through the wall of doubt, if you have it?"

"Yes, I remember that conversation."

"I believe your true passion is writing. Every time you read one of your short stories to me I felt the excitement in your voice. Do you recall me telling you that everyone in life has a destiny and God places people in the path of your life's journey and they are there for one reason?"

"Yes, ma'am."

"And for what reason are those people there?"

"You said they were there to help me find my destiny."

"I believe that writing is your destiny. You will find someone to help you."

"You sound mighty sure of yourself, Hettie."

"It's the faith and belief I have in you. Arnold, you have enough moxie to pick up the phone and call the president of Random House. You just focus on writing the story as well as you can and the publication will follow. I want the world to know about my maxims."

"Okay, you have convinced me, dear friend." At that moment I thought I would see her again so there was no need for good-byes. She asked me about my children and how they were doing. She had made my family her family, and she loved to hear stories about my daughter and son. After a few minutes we hugged. I squeezed her hand and said, "I love you, Hettie."

She said, "I love you too, Arnold."

She was asleep before I left her room.

Next Saturday I pulled into the drive-in-window of Kentucky Fried Chicken. I looked at my watch and I was on time. I chose brownies for our dessert. Her nursing home was close by and the food was always warm when I arrived. I walked into the home, but didn't see Carol anywhere. I thought she must be in one of the patient's room. I tucked the boxes under my arm and proceeded down the corridor toward Hettie's room. She wasn't sitting in her chair and I heard someone running down the hall behind me. It was Carol.

She said, "Arnold, don't go in her room."

My heart told me, "Hettie's in Heaven."

She came up to me and put her hands on my shoulders, "Mrs. Keller died an hour ago."

"Carol, please kneel with me." We knelt down in the hallway and I said a prayer, "God help us now. Give us strength and courage. Thank you for all the good times we shared with Hettie. Amen."

Carol looked at me and said, "She had been talking about you all morning. It was Arnold this and Arnold that. She kept pushing the button on her talking clock and when the voice told her the time Mrs. Keller said, 'He'll be here in two hours.' Then at 10:30 she reached up to her neck and closed her hand around the locket you gave her. She clutched it as she took her last breath."

There was a large lump in my throat, but the thought of Hettie at peace was such comfort. I stood and reached my hand for Carol and helped her up. I said, "You have to get dinner prepared for everyone. You go right along. I'm okay."

Carol hugged me and left with the boxes of chicken. I walked toward Hettie's room. The musty odor of old Braille books filled the room. Her afghan was draped over the bottom of the bed. I sat in my chair and looked around the room. Her footstool was next to her chair. A Braille book was in her chair and I reached down and picked it up. The Bible. A black ribbon marked her place. I decided to take the book with me to the Center for the Visually Impaired and have them tell me the last words she read. There was a spot on the page that looked like it had been made from something wet, maybe a tear. I circled the spot with a pencil. I remembered the first maxim she gave me," PRAYER ALWAYS WORKS. I bowed my head and prayed:

"God give me strength to deal with the loss of my dear friend, Hettie Keller, and I offer my thanks to You for bringing her into my life."

A feeling of strength came over me and the sound of Hettie's laughter filled the room. Thoughts of her flooded my mind: I remembered the Saturday I took her to Joe's grave, and I could picture Hettie sitting on the navy blue blanket; listening to the voice of Bette Midler as she sang: "The Wind Beneath My Wings." I recalled the Christmas day we spent singing songs to the tune of her harmonica. My heart was filled with one happy memory after another. I stood and walked around the room. Carol came in and asked, "I have dinner on the table. Would you care to join us?"

"No thanks, I want to spend some time alone here where we had so many happy hours together."

She walked over and we hugged. Carol said, "She was a special spirit. My life was blessed by knowing her."

"I know what you mean. By the way, there are a few of her things that I would love to have for keepsakes."

"Help yourself to anything you want. As you know she had no family." Carol reached into her pocket and pulled out the locket I gave Hettie for her birthday and handed it to me. "I'm sure you want this. I saved it for you."

I raised it to my lips and kissed the locket like Hettie did on the day I gave it to her. Then I handed it back to Carol. "Will you please see that she has it on when they bury her? She told me when I put it around her neck for the first time that she would never take it off."

Carol said, "I'll take it by the funeral home tonight and tell them. I have to get back to the others now. Please stay in touch and don't forget Chucky and I want you to come to our wedding."

"I will be there for sure and I'll stop by here and see you as often as I can."

After Carol left the room I picked up the two hugging mice that I gave her for Christmas. I took the harmonica from her nightstand and the afghan she kept on her bed. Her change purse was on the dresser and I opened it and removed a quarter for a "good luck piece." Before I left her room I sat in her wingback chair and thought, "Hettie, God led us to each other. Your love and inspiration will be with me always. Please ask God to help me write our story."

On the way home, I stopped by the Chattahoochee River and walked along the path. When I came to the place near the river where we put our feet in the water, I sat down and took off my socks and shoes. The cool water eased some of the heartbreak of the day. I thought, "RELAX WITH NATURE." I could see her with her chin raised as she said, "I promise you a life of peace and happiness if you practice these maxims."

Three weeks after Hettie's funeral, I drove into Atlanta to have someone at the Center for the Visually Impaired look at the section of the Braille Bible she was reading on the morning of her death. The ribbon bookmark was on Chapter Five of Galatians in the New Testament. The teardrop on the page that I had marked with a pencil was on verse Fourteen. The Braille reader's fingers tracked across the page and she read to me, "For the whole law is summed up in one commandment: Love your neighbor as you love yourself." I nodded and took a deep breath.

After leaving the Center I stopped by the florist and bought flowers to place on her grave. I drove to the cemetery in East Point where Joe and Hettie Keller, and her parents were buried. When I placed the last flower on Hettie's grave I remembered her saying, "Oh, Arnold. What a beautiful thought, but right now I have to go to the bathroom!" I looked over at the caretaker's house and thought about us racing toward it with Hettie saying, "Hurry!"

Hettie Keller was a true hero. Born in a Georgia cotton field she was three months premature, and she weighed less than two pounds. She lost her sight at four months, which in this day and age could have been cured. Education shaped her destiny. Her parents put her on the train by herself for the long ride to the Georgia School for the Blind. She continued her education at the Perkins Institute in Massachusetts where she completed the "The Harvard Course" that was taught by the Harvard Graduate School of Education and Perkins Institute for the Blind. She devoted her life to teaching Braille to both children and adults.

She was a musical genius who played several instruments. She was good enough to perform with a musical troupe at the fabulous Fox Theater in Atlanta. She was a wife for thirty-seven years and shared an incredible love with her husband, Joe.

She will always be my hero.

CHAPTER TWELVE

The pillow was soft and my nose was buried in it when the alarm sounded. The scent of Mary Beth's perfume was on the pillow as I reached for the clock. I looked over to see if she was still asleep, I lifted the blanket gently and eased out of bed. She had placed my clothes in the chair last night. I knelt down and prayed, "God thank you for bringing Mary Beth into my life. Please watch over my wife while I'm gone today and guide me on a safe journey."

Three months ago, Jinny brought a sack into my office and said, "A woman waiting in the reception room ask me to give you this."

I looked inside and saw an alligator made of rubber. I shouted, "Yes! Yes! Yes!" Before the last word was out, Mary Beth walked into my office wearing a black suit with a yellow blouse. She held her arms wide and we embraced. Jinny was seated on the sofa watching us. "Jinny, please give us some privacy. Please call Dr. Murphy's nurse and tell her I am officially retired." She had a big smile on her thin face as she bounced out of the room.

We sat on the sofa and Mary Beth said, "I'm really not as selfish as I have acted. I want to be with you forever."

I looked at her and said, "Let's get married." She replied with a favorite word of mine, "Absolutely!" We flew to Las Vegas that afternoon and were married before the sunset settled beyond the balcony of our hotel.

Several months later, after we finished a game of Scrabble, she said, "You have been talking for months about walking in the childhood footsteps of Hettie. Why don't you take a trip to Hart County and see if you can find her birthplace?"

"Are you a mind reader? How did you know I've been thinking about that?"

"You love challenges and I know how much it would mean to you to find her home. How long ago did she leave the farm?"

I paused to think, "Eighty-five-years ago."

Mary Beth smiled and said, "Where do you start in a search like this? Did she have any family still living in the county?"

"No, there is no one left. I'm going to start at the courthouse with her birth certificate and see if I can get an address. We had many conversations about her early years and I know the lay of the land and something about their home."

When I pulled out the driveway, I looked at the date on my watch and realized it was the fifth anniversary of the day Hettie and I met in the nursing home. I thought, "Now that's a good omen."

Ten minutes after leaving home I said to myself, "Hettie, I'm on the way to find the house you lived in as a child. Please ask God to lead me there. And by the way, I have a dozen lemons with me." Living without Hettie Keller for a year had been tough. Only the love of Mary Beth and the peace obtained from using her maxims had made it bearable.

I arrived in Hartwell, the county seat for Hart County, at 9 a.m. and went straight to the office of the Probate Court. An elderly woman with silver hair greeted me warmly when I walked into her office. "Good morning, young man. What can I do to help you?"

"Good morning," I said. "Can you look up a birth certificate for me, please?"

"Certainly, what's the name?"

"Her name was Hettie Higginbotham and she was born on July 29, 1899."

Her smile disappeared and she said, "Oh, I'm sorry, but we don't have it. The county didn't begin to record births until around 1915."

I thought, "My good chance just dropped to slim." I had no address and the family left the county long ago. Sitting down in front of her desk, I said, "How long have you been working for the Probate Court?"

She smiled and said, "I've been here forty-four years."

"That's good. I bet you know everyone in the county."

She laughed, "Not all of them, but I do know most of the people, especially if they've lived here for a long time."

I asked her if she had a few minutes to hear an interesting story and then I told her about my friend. I had noticed that the tale of Hettie Keller was magical. People loved hearing about her and I had many stories to tell. I told her I wanted to walk in her childhood footsteps. She said, "I'd love to help you find her place. What can I do?"

I had an idea. "Please give me the names, addresses and phone numbers of some people in the county that have lived here all of their lives and are eighty years or older. Of course, I'll need to talk to people who have good memories."

"OK," she said. "I'll need some time to think about it. Why don't you go across the street and have some coffee while I work on this for you?"

I thanked her and walked to the coffee shop. I thought, "What a challenge. Even if these people are eighty-five, Hettie would have left here before they were born." When I returned to her office, she had the names of seven people that might be helpful. She also gave me a county map with each person's address highlighted. I thanked her and began the pursuit with my usual optimism.

My first house was not easy. I had to dodge two pit bulls and an angry goat to reach the porch of an old codger wearing blue overalls and a red plaid shirt. Armed only with a legal pad and pen, I was no match for the threesome that chased me toward the house. After I told him about trying to find Hettie's home, he invited me in. He was eighty-seven, lived alone and could spit tobacco juice halfway across a room into a paper cup. Even though he'd never heard of Hettie, I'd stayed longer than I should have because I dreaded my sprint back to the car.

The next person on the list lived alone in a trailer along a stream, and spent her days fishing and crocheting. The inside of her home was a rainbow of colors. There were shawls, blankets, mittens and other pieces of her handiwork. The strong smell of fried fish hastened my departure. She too had never heard of my friend, but she invited me back for an afternoon of fishing.

There are two hundred and fifty-six square miles in rural Hart County and my third name and address took me along a winding country road. I kept looking at property and trying to find cotton fields. Then I thought, "The land Hettie's family farmed could have been bought by a tree grower seventy years ago. What Hettie had described to me as gentle sloping property might now be a forest of pines."

I turned off the highway and followed a dirt road for a mile or more. A large Victorian house appeared as the road came to an end. With caution I stepped out of the car and checked for dogs and goats. It was one of those Indian summer days that come along during a Georgia winter - seventy degrees and a slight breeze out of the South. I walked up the steps and a couple was sitting in a front porch swing holding hands. The aroma of fried chicken drifted out through the screen door. I glanced at my watch. It was noon.

"Good afternoon folks," I said. "I'm trying to locate a piece of property in Hart County." We introduced ourselves.

"You're just in time for dinner," the woman said. "Sit down and make yourself at home." The charming couple had been married for sixty-six years, and they were southern to the core. Their hospitality made me feel at home the minute I stepped on their porch. Five minutes later the three of us were sitting in the dining room eating Hettie's favorite meal. They had fried chicken, mashed potatoes, macaroni and cheese, and green beans. I thought, "This is another good omen. Maybe I will find her house." After a delicious meal the wife excused herself and went to the kitchen for dessert. I thought, "Don't tell me she's made a coconut cake." I smelled the warm brownies before she entered the dining room and I thought, "Close enough." The husband made a few phone calls after dinner in an effort to help me. He didn't have any luck, but I left with a full stomach and a strong feeling of optimism.

On my way to find the fourth person I stopped along a country road. Every day I always found twenty minutes to RELAX WITH NATURE. As Hettie said, "Being with nature will give your mind a rest." I walked into the woods and sat under a large water oak. The only sound came from bird songs. A few minutes later my thoughts drifted back to Hettie. I remembered sitting in her room one Saturday, looking at her and wondering, "Why is the woman so special?"

"Hettie Keller, I think you're the wisest person I've ever met."

She raised her head toward mine and said, "What a grand compliment. Thank you."

I asked her, "Please tell me the secret to your constant good nature?"

"You could not have given me a better lead in for my next maxim. It is: ATTITUDE, ATTITUDE, ATTITUDE. You have a choice in life. You can be positive or you can be negative. I have always chosen to be positive. It's the best way."

"Hettie, you had such a hard challenge by losing your sight at four months. When and how did you develop your positive attitude?"

"Good question, she said. "You don't just snap your fingers and have a positive attitude appear. You have to work at it to instill a good one."

"What can you do to improve your attitude?"

She smiled and said, "You practice some of the other maxims. One of the most important would be to EDUCATE THE MIND. Education brings confidence, and a positive attitude is the by-product of self-confidence. Another important maxim is REGULAR EXERCISE IMPROVES. When you're physically fit it increases your self-assurance and nurtures your good attitude. And of course, you ask God to enhance your outlook. Remember, PRAYER ALWAYS WORKS. But you should pray as if it were up to God and work as if it were up to you."

I got up and walked to my car while thinking about the wisdom of Hettie Keller. I glanced at my watch and it was 1:30. I had four more stops to make. The next three people I visited had never heard of Hettie. I had one last chance. His name was Mr. McClary. The directions said he owned a convenience store on the north side of town. It was 4:15 when I walked into the store and saw a beautiful blond in her early twenties sitting behind the counter. She was flipping through a "People Magazine" as fast as she chewed her gum.

I thought of one of the great metaphors by the mystery writer, Raymond Chandler. Hettie and I both loved to read him. Chandler's metaphor about an attractive woman was: "She was a blond, the kind of blond that would make a bishop kick a hole in a stain glass window."

Her blue eyes twinkled when I asked her, "Is Mr. McClary here?"

She giggled and said, "He's in the nut house."

"What bad luck," I said. "The last name on the list and the guy is in a mental institution."

She threw her head back shaking the radiant hair off of her face, "I never said nothing about him being in a mental institution. He's downtown at the "peecan house." She laughed and gave me directions to the pecan store.

I drove into town and found an old wooden warehouse that was years from a white painting. There was a crude hand-painted sign on the front of the building: "WE BUY AND SELL NUTS." The parking lot was full and when I entered I was surprised at the activity inside. The incessant chatter sounded like a flock of magpies at dusk. People held plastic bags, buckets of all sizes and colors, laundry bags, anything that could hold a lot of pecans. Everyone was talking and laughing. I felt like I had crashed a family reunion. A tall slender man wearing khaki pants and shirt came over and said, "Howdy neighbor. My name is Billy McClary."

"I'm Arnold Heflin;" we shook hands. "I stopped by to get some pecans and to ask you a few questions about a piece of property here in Hart County."

He grinned. "Help yourself to a cup of coffee and get you a handful of those shelled pecans. Let me finish weighing up these customers and I'll be with you directly."

"Thank you, sir." I poured a cup, grabbed a handful and sat down on an old church pew against the wall. The aroma of pecans reminded me of Christmas. My thoughts drifted back to the last one Hettie and I spent together. She loved playing the harmonica for me and everyone in the home. There were many things that reminded me of Hettie Keller.

Then I felt a hand on my shoulder, I looked up and saw Mr. McClary. "Now what can I do for you, young man?"

The crowd had left the store and he sat down next to me. I told him about my four-year relationship with Hettie, and how I wanted to find her birthplace.

"How many acres did they farm?" He lit his pipe.

"It was about eighty," I said. "I think it was on the eastern side of the county."

"Why's that?"

"She told me they used to go into Elberton when they went to town." Elberton was in the county east of Hart County. "She never mentioned going to Hartwell."

Mr. McClary puffed on his pipe and he looked in deep thought. "Did she ever talk about a creek on the back of the property?"

My heart fluttered. "Yes! Yes! There was a creek. She told me about it." I jumped up and spilled coffee on my pants.

He stood up and walked toward his desk. "I think I might know the farm, but I need to call Mrs. Borders. She's ninety-five-years old and lives over in Elberton."

It was hard to contain my excitement. I reached into my pocket and squeezed the quarter I had taken from Hettie's purse after she died. It was my good luck charm. I followed Mr.

McClary like a devoted cocker spaniel, and stood by the desk while he made his call.

"Mrs. Borders; this is Billy McClary," he paused for a few seconds and then said, "I'm fine and you?"

He paused and listened. He nodded and nodded. These seconds seemed like minutes and I thought, "You'd better go back out and RELAX WITH NATURE or you're going to have yourself another heart attack."

"We've got the same over here today – bet it reached seventy degrees. Mrs. Borders, do you remember a blind girl that used to live in Hart County in the early part of this century?" Then he cupped his hand over the phone and said to me, "When was she born?"

With my hand in my pocket rubbing the quarter, I said, "July of 1899."

"She was born in the summer of 1899." He looked at me again and asked, "Did she have a younger brother?"

My head must have looked like a bobble doll to him because it was going up and down so fast. "She did have a younger brother."

He relayed the information to her and said, "Yes ma'am, that's what I thought too."

The anticipation was killing me. I felt like a six-year-old boy looking for a football every morning.

He hung up the phone. He looked at me and said, "I know the property. We can be there in ten minutes. As soon I close the store we'll leave."

I felt like I had just won the lottery. I took a deep breath and thanked God. I had heard so many stories from Hettie about the farm and her early years there. I kept following him around. "What can you tell me about the property?"

"Well, the house burned back in the fifties and has never been replaced."

I was disappointed, "The house burned?"

"Don't worry, you wanted to walk in her footsteps and we'll be doing that in few minutes."

I thought about it. He was right. Mr. McClary called the owner of the property and told him we would be walking the land. He closed the nut house and we left in separate cars with me following. The sun was low on the horizon and we had maybe thirty more minutes of light. I thought, "Why didn't you bring a camera?" My car phone rang. I answered, "Hello, sweetheart. We found it! We found it! I'm on the way now to Hettie's birthplace. I'll call you back as soon as I leave here."

Mr. McClary had told me it was on the road to Elberton. His left blinker was on and my anticipation rose as we turned off the highway and onto the property. We pulled up toward the home place and stopped. I got out the car and walked toward the remains of the house. There was a lone chimney about thirty feet tall and made of old bricks. The house had been built on a slight knoll and was surrounded by five oak trees. I felt as though I was walking on hallowed ground as I made my way to Hettie's home. I looked off to the left and got chill bumps. Lying on the ground, a few feet from the chimney, was a tin roof covered with kudzu.

One day I asked Hettie, "What's your favorite day of week?"

She said, "Any night it rains."

"Why?"

"Because our home in Hart County had a tin roof, and I loved to hear the pitter-patter sound of rain hitting the roof."

The house had been built on the highest ground of the property. Except for the few trees around the chimney the entire land was cleared and still used for farming. A couple hundred yards from the back of the house there was a line of trees across the width of the land. I asked Billy, "What's back there at the tree line?"

"That's where the creek is."

I recalled the story. Hettie told me about putting her feet in the water with her family. That's where her daddy took her to RELAX WITH NATURE. When I reached the chimney I looked into the fireplace and thought, "She sat in front of a fire eating sweet potatoes in the fall while they picked cotton inside." I knelt in front of the fireplace and I could almost feel her presence. I closed my eyes and thought about the gift of our friendship and what it meant to me. When I stood up, Billy was standing near the rear of the house. He recognized my joy and left me to my thoughts.

I walked over and asked, "Where on the property would you plant watermelons?"

He pointed down a gentle slope. "Right down there in the bottomland where the soil is the richest."

I told him the story about Hettie picking a melon for her momma one evening and running back up the hill to the house. She tripped and fell. The watermelon busted and she cried. Her dog, Sarge, began to lick her face. She didn't know if he was licking it because she was crying or because he liked watermelon.

He laughed and said, "That's a funny story. I can tell ya'll were real close."

"Yes, sir. We were and we had some great times together. You don't know how much coming here means to me."

"Well, I probably don't, but I saw the look in your eyes when you got up from the fireplace. It reminded me of the look my son had when he handed me my first grandson."

I reached out and shook his hand. "Thank you for bringing me here."

"You're welcome. I'm going to head on home now, but you can stay as long as you like. You know how to get back into town, don't you?"

"I do. And thanks again."

He walked to his car and left. The sun was setting behind the tree line and there wasn't a sound in the country. I walked back to the fireplace and knelt again. I thought, "Here's where her mom braided her hair on a cold winter night. Here's where she sat with Sarge beside her. I bowed my head and thought, "Hettie, thank you for leading me here. Thank you for all the wisdom you shared with me."

I stood and walked toward the car to leave. After a few paces I turned around to have one last look at the chimney. A lone mockingbird flew in and landed on top of it. I dropped to my knees and tears of joy rolled down my cheeks and onto the ground where she sat as a child and listened to the song of her favorite bird.

I thought about holding her hand the week before she died. She had said, "Please do me a favor."

"I'll do anything for you."

"Write a story about us."

I rose from my knees and went to the car. I came back to the remains of the house with a pad and pen. I sat on a log in front of the fireplace. As the shadows lengthened, I pondered. Then I began to fulfill my promise to my dear friend. I wrote the first sentence of our story: "I saw my friend Hettie Keller every Saturday for four years, but she never saw me."

Arnold Heflin

HETTIE KELLER'S 10 MAXIMS
For Peace and Happiness

Maxim Number One	❖	PRAYER ALWAYS WORKS
Maxim Number Two	❖	RELAX WITH NATURE
Maxim Number Three	❖	LESS IS MORE
Maxim Number Four	❖	PASSION BRINGS PURPOSE
Maxim Number Five	❖	EDUCATE THE MIND
Maxim Number Six	❖	COMMUNICATION ENHANCES LIFE
Maxim Number Seven	❖	POWER IN FORGIVENESS
Maxim Number Eight	❖	REGULAR EXERCISE IMPROVES
Maxim Number Nine	❖	LOVE THY NEIGHBOR
Maxim Number Ten	❖	ATTITUDE, ATTITUDE, ATTITUDE

Arnold Heflin

AFTERWARD

"Mockingbird's Song" was based on a true story. Names have been changed on all the characters except for my beloved brother and sister along with Hettie and me. When I saw Hettie for the last time she asked me to "write a story about us." I had taken no notes or recorded any of our conversations. We had been with each other almost every week for four years and I have told this tale to the best of my recollection.

The research was done at the Perkins School for the Blind and Leader Dogs. At Perkins, I learned that Hettie had completed the Harvard Course in 1927, which was taught by Perkins and the Harvard Graduate School of Education. Leader Dogs introduced me to a trainer who taught her how to use guide dogs. All of her family and most of her friends had died before I met her. She had a keen mind and a great memory. I asked my doctor why she could remember events that occurred 90-years ago and not recall what she had for breakfast. He explained as your short-term memory declines the brain makes adjustments and your long-term memory is enhanced.

Hettie Keller never knew that a run-in with the IRS required me to perform community service and my probation office sent me to the Center for the Visually Impaired in Atlanta. They asked me what kind of person I wanted to visit and I told them to send me to someone who needed a friend the most. The community service requirements were finished in a few months. I loved Hettie Keller and continued to see her until she died.

My punishment became a great blessing because Hettie's ten maxims brought me closer to God and subsequent peace and happiness.

Arnold Heflin

ACKNOWLEDGEMENTS

A week before she died Hettie Keller asked me to "write a story about us". I thought about it for a couple of years and then I wrote the story with the help of many people.

As soon as I finished the first draft of every chapter, I called my friends Peter and Carol Brown and read it to them. Their encouragement kept me writing. Judy Campbell with Leader Dogs in Rochester, Michigan gave me insight that opened the world of the blind to me. I asked her, "Are there any trainers with Leader Dogs who worked with Hettie Keller?" She paused and said, "Yes we have one trainer who worked with her in the eighties and his name is Larry Heflin." "Heflin" is not a common name and my arms were covered with goose bumps when she told me that. I knew Hettie Keller was smiling on me from above.

Jan Seymour-Ford is the Liberian at Perkins School for the Blind and from her I learned that Hettie had completed the "Harvard Course" while she was at Perkins. Sandra Heflin, my wife of eighteen years and friend for fifty-two years always told me, "Have faith and keep writing." She did not live to see the book's completion, but her suggestion about faith was invaluable.

Others who read the manuscript and offered suggestions are:

Pam Carman, Bob Adams, Geoff Baker, Nancy and Chuck Barattini, India Benton, Jim Brechin, John Callahan, Jinny Carter, Frank Cathey, Captain George Cusick, David Cobb, Nettie Carl, Marie Corrigan, Scott Cunningham, Yvette Jacob, Judy Giglio, Brett Hunsaker, Skip Kincaid, Guy Kezirian, MD, Emily Lynch, Dick Larson, Marian Loftin, John Murphy, Lynn Murphy, Tom O'Sullivan, John Pack, George Prater, George Purpura, Robyn Rhodes, Patty Richardson, Ebit Scherl, Georgina Smith, Melissa Spur, Ione Ulinsky, Diane Urban, Jenny and Tom Watts, Pat and Tom Wilder, Kathy and George Willis, Martha Woodham, Sandra and Dave Woodward, Jean and Andy Bell, Catherine Lamar, Steve Morgan, Jamie and Ed Milton, Father Dan Stack, Lynn and George

Hart, John Kelley, Marlyn and John McGeever, Josephine Jovings, Laura Mahoney, Pam Baskette, Patricia and Lester Harris, Paul Marotte, Paul J. Wagner, Jr., Macy Sharkey, Rowland Bradford, Sammie Brown, Gordon Miller, Sandra Sweeney, Shirley Isbell, Floyd (Sonny) Weldon, Donna and Tom Clark, Wesley Cooke, Mary Lyle, Roberta and Paul Powell, James Roberts, Ann and Richard Hourdequin, Michelle Tates, Cindy Phillips, Lorette Long Inman, and Linda Alford.

I apologize to all my friends and family that I forgot to list above.

My dear sister, Ann, never waivered in her support of my writing and me. She passed the manuscript along to several of her friends and gave me the benefit of their remarks. My brother, Alan, offered encouragement after each chapter. My children Dianne and Craig always had a cheer for me as they read the chapters. My oldest granddaughter, Nicole, read the story when she was ten-years old and she laughed and cried.

Stephen Lehman of HighBridge Audio was an editor extraordinaire and his help was invaluable. Diane Turner helped me at the last moment.

Robyn Rhodes of Cartersville did the cover design.

Two gentlemen helped this story become a reality because of their expertise with computers: Nathan Underwood and Jason Oldham with Cyber Tech Café in Cartersville, GA.

Finally, my friend for forty years, Bud Gleason, was my primary reviewer and he was always spot on. Bud was a businessman, but he should have been an English teacher. After my brutal sessions with him on the first draft, I sure was glad I never had him for an instructor.

My thanks to all.

AJH July 2011

PICTURES OF HETTIE KELLER

This is a picture of Hettie Keller taken when she was 95-Years old.

This is a picture of Hettie and the author taken a
month before she died.

Hettie's first job was in Philadelphia where she taught children how to read Braille. She is standing second from the left and she is twenty-eight years old

Made in the USA
Lexington, KY
26 January 2014